WAY *of*
Crystal Healing

In the same series:

Thorsons WAY *of* **Chakras**
Caroline Shola Arewa

Thorsons WAY *of* **Meditation**
Christina Feldman

Thorsons WAY *of* **NLP**
Joseph O'Connor and Ian McDermott

Thorsons WAY *of* **Natural Magic**
Nigel Pennick

Thorsons WAY *of* **Psychic Protection**
Judy Hall

Thorsons WAY *of* **Reiki**
Kajsa Krishni Börang

Thorsons WAY *of* **Reincarnation**
Judy Hall

Thorsons WAY *of* **Tarot**
Evelyne Herbin and Terry Donaldson

Thorsons WAY *of* **Tibetan Buddhism**
Lama Jampa Thaye

Thorsons WAY *of* **Wicca**
Vivianne Crowley

Thorsons WAY *of* **Zen**
Martine Batchelor

WAY *of*
Crystal Healing

Ronald Bonewitz, PhD

Thorsons

Thorsons
An Imprint of HarperCollins*Publishers*
77–85 Fulham Palace Road
Hammersmith, London W6 8JB

The Thorsons website address is: www.thorsons.com

First published 2001

1 3 5 7 9 10 8 6 4 2

© Ronald Bonewitz 2001

Ronald Bonewitz asserts the moral right
to be identified as the author of this work

A catalogue record for this book
is available from the British Library

ISBN 0 00 710392 1

Printed and bound in Great Britain by
Martins the Printers Limited, Berwick upon Tweed

*To my great aunts Edna and Callie:
who introduced me to the magic and
mystery of crystals and minerals*

Contents

Acknowledgements

I would like to thank, yet again, Guy and Meriel Ballard. I also wish to thank several people at Thorsons I omitted to thank for their superb work on my companion book *New Cosmic Crystals*, and for their work on this book as well: my commissioning editor Louise McNamara, my editor Charlotte Ridings, Jo Ridgeway, Richard Green, Amanda McKelvie and Aislinn McCormick.

Introduction

For most of the twentieth century – and, indeed, some centuries before – science and religion have dwelt in separate houses, suspiciously peering through the curtains at one another. But the mystical side of man cannot be long locked away, and many mystical hearts beat in the bodies of pure scientists. The past 20 years, corresponding with the dawning of the Aquarian Age, have seen some of these mutual suspicions beginning to dissipate. The realization is slowly creeping upon us that science and mysticism are part of exactly the same thing; that each is describing a portion of total reality from their own viewpoint.

Although there often seems to be a conflict between science and mysticism, the scientist and the mystic seek the same thing – Truth. But until recent times, the scientist has sought the truth of the form, and the mystic has sought the truth behind the form. It is only today, particularly as recent advances in science give us an opportunity to discover that form is just a specialized arrangement of energy (which is what the mystics have been saying for thousands of years), that we at last discover common ground between the two. Writing as both a scientist and a mystic, I find no conflict between the two; nor do I believe it is any accident that the greatest advances in science are coming at a time when we are once again beginning to rediscover our spiritual roots.

I began my first crystal collection when I was six. I was a self-taught lapidary by the age of 16, and went on to university to take a degree in geology. My professional work has included gem-mining, studies of crystal chemistry (I did some early studies on the properties of ruby for lasers), and advanced studies in geochemistry, specializing in crystal chemistry. On a more esoteric level, I have been involved with crystals since 1977, when I found and cut a set of crystals for the Findhorn Community in Scotland. In the early 1980s I wrote several books under the name suggested by my first initials: Ra Bonewitz. Through the intervening years, I have been very involved in the New Age movement, and have expanded my studies to include cosmology and psychology.

Although many readers will perhaps consider themselves to be more mystically than scientifically inclined, let us not forget that were it not for rational science we would still believe the flat Earth to be the centre of the Universe.

Albert Einstein once said that knowledge is what you have left over when you have forgotten everything you have learned in school. Knowledge is an essence. And the rational side of the brain is not equipped to deal with essence – only information. To be sure, one side of the brain feeds the other. But it is the balance between the two, their right relationship that we seek. Much of what we are remembering and being told about crystals falls into the category of information. What we really seek is knowledge. To a Western mind, the distinction between the two can be difficult.

Considerable time has passed since I wrote one of the very first crystal books – time not measured in years but in the proliferation of crystal healing and, more specifically, of crystal books. Many them suggest things about crystals which are physically impossible.

WAY of

There is a chapter in this book specifically devoted to those claims, and how they are misleading to the practicioner seeking true healing. I hope to demystify the entire process and help you get directly to your healing goals without a great deal of energy-wasting mumbo jumbo in the process!

Everything in this book works – it has done for me, it has done for many others, and it will do for you, too.

Ronald Arthur Louis (Ra) Bonewitz
England, 2000

ONE

THE MINERAL
Kingdom

Sons of the Cosmos; Brothers of Stars; Children of the Universe – so the songwriters describe the race of man. There is truth as well as poetry in these lyrics, and the questions and implications raised are all part of the greater question of the relationship between matter, spirit and man. As we shall discover, we are indeed Children of the Universe, and Brothers of Stars – and one thing the songwriters have thus far missed: Cousins of Crystals.

This is not a book about esoterics, yet esoterics cannot be separated from matter and minerals, as they are one and the same. The Mineral Kingdom is by far the first and oldest Kingdom in the Universe, and if we accept the premise that the formation of the Universe is a creative act of God, then what we discover in the Mineral Kingdom must have a great deal to do with what God had in mind as He[1] began the act of creation that led first to minerals and, finally, to men.

Some Clarity About Crystals

Crystals are about clarity – clarity of form, clarity of energy balance, clarity of purpose, clarity of thought and intention about their use – so we need to be clear about what crystals do and don't do from the very beginning. Much of this book is about sorting fact from fiction, both about crystals themselves, and about their role in the healing process.

Way of Crystal Healing focuses on the two parts of the title; the *way* crystals can be tools for *healing*. Crystal healing is a specific

---

[1] The author recognizes that God is beyond gender and is, in fact, *everything*. The word 'He' is used purely as a convention.

application of crystals, separate and distinct from divination, meditation, energizing plants, and the other uses to which crystals are put. Crystals have mainly been used in healing, but they have often been used within the paradigm of orthodox medical practice, as if they are 'medicines' to be dispensed: take a citrine for an upset stomach, or amethyst for a headache … However, crystals rightly belong in an area of practice called *energy healing*; that is, working with the body in its pure energy levels. Dispensing crystals on the basis of *physical* symptoms is working with them entirely from the wrong end. Physical manifestation of ill health – disease – is often the result of disturbances in the energy bodies, and any given physical manifestation can be the result of a number of different energetic causes. So the first principle of crystal healing must be: treat the *cause*, not the *symptom*. Clearly, this requires a shift in thinking, and it is that shift in thinking that this book is intended to address. Thus you will not find lists of diseases and lists of crystals that 'cure' them. You *will* find ways of determining where disturbances in the energy field lie, and how to go about finding the appropriate crystal to aid the patient in their *own effort* at recovery, which is where true healing is found.

However, the point we need clarity about most of all is this: *crystals do not heal*. This is an extraordinary statement to make at the very beginning of a book about crystal healing, but it is so. There is, however, much more to it beyond this simple statement, which seems to be contradicted by the thousands of crystal users who have experienced healing through contact with crystals. And, that is perfectly true. Confused? Let's follow the above statement with a further one: crystals are powerful *tools* of healing, when they are used through *human consciousness and intention* as part of the healing equation.

So, what do crystals *do*?

By themselves, *nothing*. A crystal is a tool, like a hammer – but a tool for energy. Left alone, the hammer drives in no nails; left alone, the crystal does the same – nothing. Tools only 'do' something when there is an input of human energy – with a hammer, muscle power and the mental concentration and intention to drive a nail into a piece of wood; with a crystal, the power of human consciousness and the clear intention for healing.

But, don't crystals (as many believe, and teach) 'give off' healing rays or energy? No, they don't and, moreover, they *can't*. Crystals (and hammers) exist at a level of consciousness where intention and motivation to act beyond the boundaries of their own physical, chemical and electrical dimensions simply do not exist. Beyond this, there are some very good reasons why it is a physical impossibility for crystals to 'give off' energy – healing or otherwise – which will be explained in the following chapters. But, paradoxically, within these *same* reasons we find the reasons why crystals are superb *tools* of healing, and we also find out much about the nature of our own human organism, and the natural world of which it is a part.

The Background of Crystal Healing

In the past two decades, we have experienced the growth of 'crystal consciousness' – an awareness of the life of the Mineral Kingdom. But this is a reawakened awareness which has very deep roots. The ancient Egyptians, Babylonians and Assyrians have bequeathed us a legacy that began as the use of colour in healing. The colours originally used were those that the disease being treated caused in the body: yellow jaundice, blue lips, red haemorrhage.

Because these civilizations were unable to separate the colours of the spectrum by other means, they used naturally coloured materials. Flowers and plants, white oil, red lead, red ochre, black lizards, indigo and verdigris – a copper carbonate that was mixed with wax to treat cataracts – were all used. Particularly prized were transparent stones in intense colours, valued not for themselves, but specifically for their colours: yellow beryls were used to treat jaundice, bloodstones for haemorrhages, lapis lazuli for the blue of restricted circulation, with diamond considered a cure-all, prized for its brilliance. They were, effectively, the first gemstones, worn not for adornment but for colour healing.

Until relatively recently, colour was the primary characteristic of how crystals were categorized and studied: all the red ones went in one box, all the blue ones in another, and so on. The problem was, most of the red ones had totally different shapes, hardness, lustre and ways of breaking. Aside from colour, they had little else in common with each other. So it was with the blue ones, the green ones, and so on. When reliable chemical analysis became possible in around 1800, it was also discovered that crystals of the same colour were chemically different from each other. Some of the confusion from that early time still carries forward into the healing uses of crystals today, as many of the healing uses attributed to them date to times when it was difficult to tell one crystal from another. So when we read in an old text that 'ruby' has certain uses, we don't know whether it is referring to actual ruby, one of several types of garnet, or spinel – all of which were called 'ruby' at one time or another. In fact, the huge Black Prince's Ruby in the English crown jewels wasn't discovered to be a spinel until mid-Victorian times. One presumes that Queen Victoria was not amused. In another example, the word 'sapphire' was applied to many blue stones, and in ancient texts 'sapphire' probably refers to lapis lazuli.

Clearly, when we find 'healing' uses of crystals that derive from old texts, there is a problem: exactly what were the ancient healers actually using? There is, of course, no way to know. But, as we will discover, this isn't really a problem at all. We have moved on a great deal both in our understanding of crystals and minerals, and of the disease process.

Crystals and the Mineral Healing

Crystals are everywhere. They come in many sizes, shapes and colours. Some crystals are organic, created through biological processes. Some are inorganic, created through the forces of nature – from the centres of stars to the inner world of planetary chemistry; and some are created in the laboratory, with no equivalent in the natural world. So what, exactly, is a *crystal*. Definitions vary from the poetic – the Flowers of the Mineral Kingdom – to the more precise: *order* and *form*. The atoms of crystals are arranged in immensely precise, repeating patterns, and, as a consequence of those inner patterns, they have an outer pattern that is in some way a reflection of the inner. These outer patterns are forms that occur in geometry – cubes, octahedrons, dodecahedrons, and so on.

There is another state of matter where atoms are still in precise arrangements, but because of the conditions under which their arrangements occurred, there were no opportunities for the corresponding external forms to develop. This state of matter is called *crystalline*. It is a fairly common state of solid matter – much more common than crystals. Within the crystalline state are the enamel of your teeth, the microscopic structure of your bones, the ice in your drink, the metal in your car.

When we speak of crystals for healing, we almost always refer to crystals formed in the natural world of the Mineral Kingdom. Yet many crystals are artificially grown, so why don't we use these? If you ever have the chance to hold a synthetic crystal, see how it feels. Or even better, hold it in one hand and a natural one of the same mineral in the other. The vast majority of people doing this experiment will say that the natural one feels 'alive', the synthetic one lifeless, clinical – rather like the laboratory in which it was grown. Both crystals are absolutely identical mineralogically to one another, yet the synthetic one feels like a lump of glass. This is a dramatic demonstration of the fact that there is a 'consciousness' involved in the creation of the Mineral Kingdom that is both alive and of which we are capable of being aware. Does this mean there is some little entity living in each crystal? No. But it does mean that there is a dimension of Universal Consciousness that finds expression through the Mineral Kingdom. It can be reasonably stated that the Mineral Kingdom is, ultimately, the foundation for all life, both on the Earth and beyond.

Our own bodies are made entirely of minerals: about half a bathtub of the molten form of the mineral ice, and a few handfuls of carbon, calcium, potassium, magnesium, a couple of cubic yards (a metre or so) of oxygen, and a thimbleful of a dozen or so other elements – all derived from the Mineral Kingdom. We are, in a sense, nothing more than evolved minerals.

How much mineral matter does the human race embody? An average human body will fit into a box 12 inches (30cms) deep, 18 inches

(45cms) wide, and less than 6 feet (2m) high. The entire human race fills a cube with sides measuring just over half a mile long; a moderate-sized lake of water, about enough to supply London or New York for a couple of weeks or so in a hot summer; and a very small hill of other minerals.

Yet just look at the changes wrought on the face of the Earth by that lake of water and mound of chemicals embodied in the human race. This should give us an idea of how a relatively small portion of the human race can affect positively the world around us. As we develop our own inner clarity, and work with the Earth from that clarity, we get powerful results. Clear intentions get clear results – if you have no real intentions, you get no real results.

This is also a very powerful demonstration of the theme of this book: the power of healing is in the hands of none other than ourselves. We can use appropriate tools – like crystals – but ultimately the power lies within each and every one of us.

The Origin of the Mineral Healing

Part of the broader understanding both of the Mineral Kingdom and its crystals and the disease process in the human body, derives from understanding the origins of both the crystals and our own bodies, for they are exactly the same. The Universal Mind which created crystals also created us, and both man and minerals are part of the *same* thought. Both are part of the internal processes of the universe itself and manifestations of its own highest Consciousness, which is often referred to as 'God'. But crystals do what they do however we define 'God'.[2] Setting definitions aside, we will take a closer look at the processes themselves.

The Mineral Kingdom – and everything else in the universe – was born in the same instant in the event called the Big Bang. Twelve to fifteen thousand million years ago, the entire universe was confined in a sphere about the size of a *pea* – or even smaller. Literally every single thing that exists in the universe today was there in that tiny ball of energy: every star, every moon, every planet, every atom in your body, what you ate for breakfast, every thought you will ever think, every feeling you will ever feel – and most of all, *you*. What is energy? In purely scientific terms, we do not know, but we do know that everything in the universe is made from it. And at the moment of the Big Bang – that great expansion of the little ball of energy to become the universe – that energy began its journey to evolve into other forms: particles like protons and electrons, atoms, molecules, minerals, planets and, eventually, people.

One-hundredth of a second into the Big Bang, the temperature of the embryonic universe cooled to about 100 thousand million degrees centigrade, and basic particles condensed in large amounts from that energy, although the universe was still just a broth of particles, energy and radiation. The universal broth at that point was still so dense that a thimbleful would be as heavy as a mountain range on today's Earth.

The four basic particles created in the first moments of the universe's new life were *photons* – light, *neutrinos* – particles so small they pass right through the Earth without hitting anything, *electrons*

[2] A detailed description of the universal processes and their relationship to Higher Consciousness may be found in my book *New Cosmic Crystals* (Thorsons, 2000).

– negatively charged particles, and *positrons* – positively charged electrons. As further cooling took place over the next ten seconds, all of these new particles began to bind together to form simple atomic nuclei. In many esoteric writings we read that the Universe and all within it are made from 'light', which is, if taken literally, not so. Light particles (photons, carriers of electromagnetism) make up only a quarter of the basic particles from which the universe is built!

After a few minutes had passed, the universe cooled further to a thousand million degrees centigrade – about seventy times hotter than the centre of the sun, and by then all of the fundamental relationships which shape the universe and everything in it – including you – were set in motion. But another 70,000 years of cooling needed to pass before the nuclei could begin to capture electrons to form atoms. The first and only atoms which formed at that stage were atoms of hydrogen, the lightest and simplest of all atoms, and relatively few of the available particles combined. Probably due to uneven cooling, the hydrogen began to separate and concentrate in vast, more compact clouds, where gravity began to draw in yet more hydrogen. In the centres of the clouds even more compacting occurred, which in turn increased the gravity, drawing in yet more gas. As the flow of gas toward the centre increased the clouds started to rotate, setting up whirls and eddies, where hotspots began to develop within their centres. More compaction and heating occurred as yet more gas was drawn in, until the gas at the centre became so hot and dense that the atoms of hydrogen began to stick together, fusing to create helium. This fusion released the photons (light particles) bound up in the fusing atoms, and the first stars were born.

As hydrogen fuses to form helium and release light, more heat is released, causing the centres of stars to become even hotter and raising the pressures higher; at which point helium begins to fuse to itself to form even more complex atoms such as carbon, oxygen, iron, silicon and other, heavier elements. This cycle eventually reaches a state of equilibrium where the gravity of the contracting centre holds the expansion into heat and light exactly in balance, and so it stays for the life of the star. When enough of the hydrogen supply is used up, the equilibrium of the star becomes unbalanced, and it either collapses inward on itself or explodes into a supernova – the two forms of star death.

In the beginning of the universe, and even now since the universe is a relatively young place, the majority of stars were hydrogen-rich. Hydrogen-rich stars explode, expanding as they die, to scatter their core of heavy elements and their remaining hydrogen back into the broth of the universe. It is at the stage of explosive star-death that the very heaviest elements are created: uranium, platinum, gold, and so on. Hydrogen-poor stars contract, collapsing inward to become more compact stars – white dwarfs. Eventually white dwarfs collapse again to become neutron stars, and finally again to become black holes: matter so dense that it begins to approximate the original density before the Big Bang.

In the autumn and winter skies in the northern hemisphere you can see stars being born: The Pleiades – seven visible stars surrounded by a dimly-lit gas cloud, the cloud from which they are contracting. If you had walked the earth 70,000 years ago as our ancestors did, there would have been nothing to see. They are that new. Stars younger than Man.

The very first minerals were formed from the scattered remnants of the first stars to die in supernova explosions, formed from the 'dust' that was the remains of their cores. Most of the dust was too small

11

to be seen – literally a cloud of single atoms. Because of the varying degrees of atomic attractiveness, the atoms selectively began to connect with each other, and the first patterns they formed connected themselves to like patterns of identical chemical composition – the first mineral atomic 'cells'. These were the tiny bits of solid matter that accumulated around newly forming stars, building planets and moons – and finally, the Earth. Our Sun is a third-generation star, a star made up of the remnants of two earlier phases of star birth and death. Two other generations of stars have lived and died to supply the material for our sun, its brothers and sisters, and their moons and planets.

Around our newly-forming sun, as around countless other suns, the heavier dust particles were drawn by gravity into a flat disc shape, where they began to collide with themselves to form larger particles. Scattered dust collected as sand grains; sand grains collided to become pebbles; pebbles merged to become boulders; boulders accumulated by gravity to become planets and moons. In this manner the Earth and the other planets of our solar system formed. Our own Moon – and possibly others – was formed when a large object (probably the size of a small moon itself), collided with the Earth during its period of accumulation. The material hurled from the primal Earth eventually settled into orbit, and was again drawn together by gravity to coalesce into the Moon. On the newly formed Earth, new processes began, processes that continue to this day. They are the processes of a living planet, and one of their products is crystals – as we discover in Chapter 3.

But this is science.[3] Do we have any evidence for such cosmic events in mythology, in the intuitive understanding of the deeper

[3] My personal definition of science is that it is *'the branch of mysticism dealing with the measurable'.*

undercurrents running through all of creation? It turns out that we do.

Cosmic Mythology

From China we discover in the P'an Ku myths:

> *First there was the great cosmic egg. Inside the egg was chaos, and floating in chaos was P'an Ku, the Undeveloped, the divine Embryo and P'an Ku burst out of the egg, four times larger than any man today, with a hammer and chisel in his hand with which he fashioned the world.*[4]

In Hinduism, we find the belief that the Cosmos itself undergoes an infinite series of deaths and rebirths. In the Hindu belief system, there are a number of time scales that correspond rather well to our current concept of the universe. Its cycles run from our ordinary day and night, to a day and night of Brahma, which is 8.64 thousand million years long. This is longer than the age of the Earth or the Sun, and about half the time since the Big Bang. The Universe, then, is the dream of a god who, after a hundred Brahma years, dissolves himself into dreamless sleep; after another hundred Brahma years, he awakens and recomposes himself, to once again dream the cosmic dream. At the beginning of each cosmic cycle, the creation of the universe is represented as the cosmic dance of Shiva in his manifestation as the Dance King. In this manifestation, Shiva's upper right hand (he has four) holds a drum whose sound is the sound of creation. In his upper left hand is a tongue of flame, a reminder that

---

[4] Quoted in *Cosmos*, by Carl Sagan.

the newly created universe will, billions of years from now, be utterly destroyed.

These images, both Chinese and Hindu, are thousands of years old, but are they so unlike the conclusions of modern science? Every religion and belief-system accepts that the formation of the universe was a deliberate act by some form of Creator, so can we simply not accept that the Big Bang merely represents the physical outworking of the fact of creation?

The Mineral Kingdom can be seen as the 'backbone' of the universe. While its most prominent denizens are the stars which swirl in the galaxies, there is still an insubstantialness about them – they are, after all, just large balls of gas. Minerals, whether as disparate dust particles or as planets, have rigid structures and long-term stability. While their structures may change as a result of geological conditions, they change only into other stable and fixed forms. Thus in a universe of emerging form, they are the first fixed and stable forms upon which all other forms eventually develop.

How is all of this connected to healing? First and foremost is the recognition of the fact that it *is* connected, because everything in the Universe is energy. Not just energy as matter, but energy as thought, energy as emotion, energy as experience. Healing *must* be some type of energy, because *everything* is.

You, and all that you embody, are patterns of universal energy. When those patterns become disturbed for whatever reason, then at some level the patterns of the universe itself are disturbed. Is it any wonder then, that an urgent need arises to call your attention to that fact? When all else fails, the message comes through loud and clear in a way that cannot be ignored. It is called *disease*.

TWO

HOLISTIC HEALING/
Holistic Health

Until we fully understand the word 'health', there is little point in talking about 'healing', for what is the point of healing except to bring about a higher state of health? There has been a tendency, even in complementary practice, to define health in terms of the absence of disease. But the nature of disease itself – particularly in the Western world – has been misunderstood. Both of these failures of comprehension lie within the failure to understand the nature of *life*.

To fully comprehend the principles behind both healing and health, it is useful to restate the First Principle: it is *all* energy. Recently in the West, fortunately, there has been an increasing acceptance of the idea that the human body is more than just flesh; that it has components that are purely energetic in nature – energies that are the manifestation of Universal energies. Ultimately, because *everything* is energy, including the very atoms and molecules of your body, the consequence is that your body – like everything else in the universe – must obey the fundamental laws of energy. And the most fundamental of those laws is that energy always seeks to balance itself. In the centres of stars, when the heat and pressure get too great, atoms fuse together to create new atoms that are stable in the new environment; their energies reach a new balance. In the Mineral Kingdom, as we will discover, atoms combine to form new structures in order to create balance, and crystals form. In your own body – inseparable from your mind, emotions and spirit, which are, ultimately, just different levels of energy – when one or more of those components gets out of sync with the greater whole, one or more of the other components must shift to compensate. Illness – physical, mental, emotional or spiritual – is the result.

Disease is not just a malfunction of the physical body, which tends to be treated in orthodox practice as if it were nothing more than an organic machine. The human organism is made of many inter-woven and interlinked facets, some of which are physical but others of which – as complementary practitioners have long understood – are purely energetic.

Many healing therapies such as acupuncture, acupressure, reiki, the laying on of hands – and crystal healing – are all built on the premise that the body's energy flows can be influenced in a positive way through outside intervention. This in turn is based on the understanding that the body's energetic nature is both reflected in and influences the functioning of the physical body.

Holistic Health

Holistic healing is a term most readers will be familiar with; but how often do we hear its complementary term: holistic *health*? Despite its recognition of the energetic nature of the human organism, com-plementary practice has still tended to follow many of the patterns set down by orthodox medicine, rather than evolve new patterns of thinking more in keeping with the nature of its practice. As noted, orthodox medicine tends to define health in terms of disease – in other words, its absence. *Holistic health* is more than the absence of disease – it is the full integration into a unified whole of body, mind and spirit. Further, it is the recognition that if any one of these aspects is 'unhealthy' – i.e., out of balance with the whole – then the whole itself is unhealthy. Orthodox medicine has always had a prob-lem defining health in its own terms, in that having developed out of the Western, scientific paradigm, wherein the concept of holism, and especially the idea that *spiritual* health is part of the equation, simply doesn't exist.

Further, the idea that all three of these aspects act as a unified whole, and moreover, *are* a unified whole, whether healthy or not, is still lacking even in much of complementary healing practice. Because mind, body and spirit are a unified whole, it becomes an impossibility to reach total health unless all three aspects are treated, for the simple reason that all three are not only interactive with each other, but they are *at the same time one with each other*, and *reflections of* each other.

When we understand that the human organism is a whole entity, whose interpenetrating and interacting components are mind, body and spirit, the next understanding becomes easier: that, within the whole organism, there is a set of priorities that relate to different aspects of the organism. In simpler terms, the spirit and all that relates to the spirit – the human dimension often referred to as the soul – is necessarily the dimension to which the other dimensions must ultimately be subordinate. The growth and development of the soul is, in the end, all that really matters. This is not to say that other needs may not be more pressing in the moment, but even these needs are, in the end, part of that One, ultimate goal. To the starving, nothing matters but food; to the freezing, nothing matters but warmth. Yet these powerful drives are themselves creations of the One need: if the body perishes, the learning vehicle is lost, and the soul must start again with another one.

The Roles of the Body and Illness

When we can recognize that the body is, in the end, a creation of the soul's need for growth, then it follows that all that has occurred in our lives to bring us to our current state of physical, mental and emotional being is the outworking of our own personal plan for growth. The messages our physical body sends us through its illnesses, feelings and emotions are clear pointers to help us heal those inner divisions within us that keep us from being the perfect embodiment of the spirit that dwells inside us – if we are able to listen to and correctly interpret these messages.

There can be no true healing until the nature of disease itself is understood. In the Western world generally, our failure to comprehend both the *nature* and *role* of disease is the direct result of our failure to perceive its role in the wider picture: the relationship of the human species to the greater whole of the natural world. Holistic healers in particular need to realize that the *relief of symptoms* is not *healing*. You can take aspirin for a headache, but it does nothing to treat the brain tumour causing the pain. You can use a crystal to relieve a symptom, but unless an inner shift happens toward a more complete alignment of body, mind and spirit, real healing hasn't taken place. The good news about *crystal* healing is that this often happens as a direct result of the inner-directed healing process of the patient themself, and happens whether the healer – or patient[1] – are even aware of it. It is, in fact, one of the most powerful and vital responses when crystals are used in the healing process. In a later chapter (Chapter 6), the idea of 'mirroring' is introduced. Because crystals are the fundamental patterns of creation, all that we embody within ourselves must also harmonize with and reflect those patterns. In the presence of crystals the inner part of ourselves that knows and responds to the need for balance is bolstered and

---

[1] In this text the word 'patient' is used to designate the person undergoing treatment. In many complementary practices the term 'client' is preferred. 'Patient' is used herein solely because it is a more commonly recognized term.

activated. Thus crystals become the perfect mirror for the very processes we exist to undertake.

The ultimate need, then, is to reharmonize ourselves to our deepest inner being, the soul-level of existence. Our attention is called to the need to do this in many ways: failed relationships, unhappiness at work, feelings of emptiness and isolation, and dissatisfaction with the accomplishments and material gains our society tells us are important. Our physical bodies have their own method of drawing attention to the necessity for reharmonization – disease. Illness is ultimately about healing the soul, about healing the real you. Illness is not something wrong with you; *it is a message about the state of your inner harmony.* Illness is something that your body is trying to tell you to help you get right, to heal you at a very profound level. Illness is a symptom of something much deeper. It is a pointer to the need for change, change that brings you into greater alignment with the real purpose of your life: to achieve a greater state of one-ness with all of creation. Because illness is a symptom, to simply remove the symptom itself creates no real healing. Unless the underlying cause is discovered and dealt with, the disease process just repeats itself somewhere else, in some other form.

Disease and the body

Australian doctor John Harrison has been a pioneer in the recognition that disease is a result of inner factors. He says:

> *Disease is both self-created and self-cured. Illness
> is the physical and psychological result of unre-
> solved needs, not a malfunction of a machine
> caused by unknown or external factors.*[2]

[2] John Harrison, M.D. *Love Your Disease* (London: Angus and Robertson, 1984) p.4.

His work demonstrates that unless the underlying psychological causes (which are themselves manifestations of deeper spiritual needs) are dealt with, the disease process simply repeats itself elsewhere. But he also emphasizes that this understanding of the disease process is very hopeful: as we become more and more familiar with our own investment in developing diseases, we can begin to assume more and more control over our disease and, finally, over our personal destiny – in other words, finally to become who we really are.

Another doctor, Dr Richard Moss, pioneered the idea that the disease process also relates to various levels of energy. At the lowest energy level are the diseases that are clearly separate entities from ourselves, like viruses and bacteria, easily distinguishable from our own body, and which *cause* malfunctions of the body, rather than *are* malfunctions of the body. High-energy diseases, like cancer and heart disease, are direct cellular breakdowns, and are direct malfunctions of the body, as opposed to invasions of the body by outside organisms.

The high-energy diseases *begin* in the energy levels, and occur when we are out of balance with our own highest energy level – the soul level. They are a result of deep-level conflict between our ideas about living, and our own inner knowledge of how we *should* be living. The prominent high-energy diseases indicate an extremely deep level of inner conflict, creating enormous stress at the cellular level, which, when combined with the numerous toxins available in our environment, produce cellular breakdown. About the development of cancers, Dr Moss says:

> *We would like to continue believing that the*
> *human immune system ... has all of a sudden*

stopped functioning, and allowed the development
of the tumour ... In fact, the human immune
system may not be failing. Perhaps it is simply
not subtle enough to recognize the force it is
dealing with.[3]

The 'force it is dealing with' is the force generated by our separation from the natural lifestyle that our biology intends us to live. What we are often really missing is the connection to an essential part of ourselves, that part of us that exists as an integral part of the natural environment.

Healing and the 'Placebo Effect'

Although the 'placebo effect' is well known to medical practitioners and researchers alike, its true nature seems to have been overlooked. It is considered to be one of the most difficult factors to 'eliminate' from medical trials. It means, in effect, that a certain percentage of patients – up to *60* percent in some trials – will get well as long as they think they are receiving medication – even if they are in fact receiving so-called 'sugar pills', containing no medicine whatsoever. This is both good news and bad news, depending on whether you are an orthodox practitioner or a complementary practitioner. In the absence of the kind of controls used in medical research – which are impossible anyway, due to the nature of the treatment, there is no *scientific* evidence that crystal healing works.[4] Indeed, one writer critical of crystal healing stated that it was *all* due

---

[3] Richard Moss, M.D. *The I That is We* (Berkeley: Celestial Arts, 1981) p.57.
[4] Apropos of this, there is no *scientific* evidence that love, kindness, joy, brotherhood or loyalty exist either.

to placebo effect. This is the 'bad' news. The good news is that there are plenty of recorded cases of crystal healing. The writer knows of one practitioner in Holland who has reported over *ten thousand* healings. Can this all be placebo effect? Probably not, but even if it is, the good news is, *so what*?

That the human mind has the ability to heal its own body is well enough known in medical circles, and there is even an entire branch of medicine/psychology devoted to it – or more specifically, to the interaction between the mind and the body's immune system. It is called *psychoneuroimmunology*. What has been 'discovered' is that the mind and body operate as a single unit, and that the old division into mind *and* body is an entirely artificial one. This will hardly be news to complementary, holistic practitioners, who have been saying this all along, but at least science is, to a degree at least, finally catching up. Further, it is being revealed that many of the processes which take place in the body/mind to initiate and facilitate healing are entirely unconscious. It, therefore, may not be too much of a leap to suggest that perhaps the inner reactions of the body/mind that create the so-called 'placebo effect' are, in fact, the body's *natural and preferred* method for healing itself. And, that those who do not respond in this way to the healing process – those who require medication – are those in whom the natural healing mechanism is blocked in some way.

Energy Blockages

Blocks are established in the physical body and in our body energy centres through traumatic childhood events, or even while we are in the womb. The psychological term for this process is *repression*, and it is the body's way of shunting the biochemical results of trauma into the body's cells at a time when their effects on the body – highly elevated heart rate, dramatically increased metabolism of sugar, and overload of adrenaline – could prove fatal, particularly in the case of infants. And there the results of the trauma stay, undermining the immune system and ultimately resulting in disease – which is one way of releasing all the trapped energy – or until other life situations occur where it can begin to be safely (at least in the life-threatening sense) released. This is what happens in later life when events occur that trigger strong emotional responses, sometimes out of all proportion to the actual events that 'caused' them.

Not only are our physical and emotional bodies affected, but our mental body is as well; as, indeed, we would expect of a holistic system. 'Mental' problems, like neurosis, have their beginnings in the repression response as well, and have their physical counterparts. It is a system out of balance with itself.

However, simply being told that these blockages and the conflicts that created them exist does not resolve them. There is energy locked up in the body, and the only way we can discharge it is to experience it. Primal Therapy and Bioenergetics are but two of a number of therapies which have evolved specifically to address such conflicts, and to create a physical environment where these energies can be safely let out. In the process, we can make a perceptual shift in ourselves, and thereby resolve and release the conflicts at all levels.

Crystals have a role to play in this process. They can be very useful for this work because both the blockages and the conflicts which created them are energetic in nature. The unified mind/body/spirit is a being that is ultimately all energy, including the 'solid' matter of our physical body.[5] The energetic bodies that are a part of the physical body not only penetrate it, but extend far beyond it. It is this field of energy that is experienced as the *aura*.

The Aura

As Ted Andrews notes:

> *The aura is the energy field that surrounds all matter. The atoms of animate life are more active and vibrant than those of inanimate matter. Thus the energy fields of trees, plants, animals and people are more easily detected and experienced.*[6]

And, of course, at the slowest level of vibration, there exists the energy field of minerals.

Many, if not most people would say that they don't 'see' auras, but Andrews points out that we continually sense them, although we seldom recognize that that is what we are doing. These are some of the questions he asks, all of which are ways of sensing the aura:

> 1   *Have you ever felt when someone was staring at you, or had an instant liking or disliking for someone?*

---

[5] See the discussion of the atom in Chapter 3.
[6] Ted Andrews, *How to Read the Aura* (St Paul: Llewellen, 1998) p.2.

> 2 *Have you ever been able to sense how*
> *someone is feeling, in spite of how this person*
> *was acting?*

> 3 *Have you ever walked into a room and*
> *tightened up, fidgeted or felt angry? Do some*
> *rooms make you want to stay? Or make you*
> *want to leave?*[7]

The other classic experience, which most of us have had at some time or another, is to ignore a first impression, only to find that it bears itself out eventually!

There are numerous other experiences that all of us have almost on a daily basis, that are interactions with our own aura and that of other people, places or things, but that we never identify as being such.

The aura is part of the whole field of energy that makes up the human being, and helps explain why energy healing is possible. Part of the auric makeup is the projection of our own consciousness. When crystals are brought into the aura, they interact with it. But what do they actually *do*? Essentially, crystals do nothing more than mirror what is already there – all of the things which are part of you, including some things which you might not be aware of about yourself. Within each and everyone of us – more deeply buried in some than in others – is the ability to heal: to bring about a state of perfect balance and harmony at all levels. The crystal is an archetype of perfect balance and harmony. Thus we *recognize* in the crystal, that which *already* exists within us. We couldn't recognize it if it

[7] Ibid, p.3.

wasn't already within us. However, many people mistakenly believe that what we experience in the crystal belongs to the crystal, rather than to us – so out of touch are many of us with those dimensions of ourselves. Thus the crystal is perceived as giving off healing energy – when what we are really experiencing is our own inner-healing ability reflected back to us.

The aura and its expression through the chakras, acupuncture meridians and energy healing generally, is part of an understanding that the mind, body and spirit exists both as part of and as a field of energy in its own right.[8] Moreover, the energy which the aura is part of is the energy of the Earth and the Cosmos. Within the levels of energy we embody there exists a 'spectrum' of energies. At one extreme are the denser, purely physical energies that relate to the world of matter and reproduction (and often described as 'dense' energies), while at the other are the 'highest' level energies: those of the spirit – lighter, subtle, refined, and easily overlooked in the hurly-burly of everyday life. Between these extremes are five other levels, each relating to a different level and dimension of life. Various religions and philosophies have given names to these different yet interconnected levels and dimensions of energy, and the treatment carried out by an energy healer will be a consequence of his or her own understanding of this greater whole. Crystal healing is part of this understanding. As we will discover, the energies that crystals embody are part of the energetic environment in which the human body evolved.

Although we don't know exactly what energy is, we can measure its properties as heat, as light, as atomic forces, and equally, when we work with energy *healing*, we can observe its effects without

[8] The subject of chakras and chakra balancing is explored in Chapter 10.

precisely defining what it is. How we observe its effects and how the body responds to treatment depends to some degree on what we are looking for. An acupuncturist looks for the lines of energy flow within the body – called meridians – that have been defined through hundreds of years of practice, knowing that the placement of needles at certain places within that flow has an observable influence on the physical body (see Figure 1). Acupressure does the same, but uses pressure at critical points rather than needles. Other therapies that use massage techniques work on essentially the same principles.

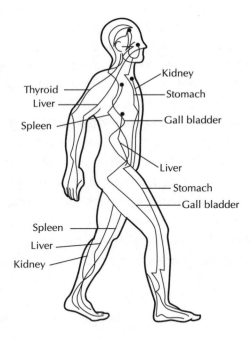

Figure 1: Energy meridians and acupuncture points

The Effect of Crystals

To summarize what we have discussed thus far, let us ask the question: what exactly do crystals do?

To answer this, we must be very careful about the word *do*. To some, it can mean that the object acts of its own choice and volition – a widely held view of crystals. But what do crystals really do? By themselves, *nothing*. As noted in Chapter 1, a crystal is a tool, like a hammer, which can only have an effect through somebody's conscious intention. However, a crystal is a tool for energy.

As was also noted, many readers will have heard that crystals somehow 'give off' 'healing energy'. This is physically impossible. A crystal is in a perfect state of equilibrium – that is, neither giving off energy nor taking it in. If it were taking in energy, it would be growing; if it were giving off energy, it would be shrinking. Therefore crystals do not – and *cannot* – sit there giving off 'healing energy'. It is one of the many myths about crystals that will be explored in Chapter 5.

But …

Many healers are working with crystals, and many 'healings' take place. If the crystal isn't giving off some sort of energy, what is it that is happening? The answer to that question is precisely the purpose of this book, because within that answer is the answer to more than just the question of crystal healing: it is the answer to the nature of life itself, and how we live and experience it on and as part of the Earth. Through this we have an opportunity not only to learn much more about our own lives but, using our new knowledge, to live our lives more richly and fully.

WAY of

The great Mystical scholar Joseph Campbell wrote about the quest for health and wholeness:

> *People say that what we're all seeking is a meaning for life. I don't think that's what we're really seeking. I think what we're seeking is an experience of being alive, so that our life experiences on the purely physical plane will have resonances with our innermost being and reality, so we can feel the rapture of being alive.*[9]

It is to this end that all healing – especially crystal healing – is oriented; not just to the fulfilment of some cosmic purpose in the future, but in full and joyous aliveness in the here and now.

[9] Joseph Campbell, *The Power of Myth* (London: Doubleday, 1988).

THREE

THE STRUCTURE
of Crystals

The reason for taking a look at the physical makeup and structure of crystals is simple: *crystals do what they do because they are what they are.*

The standard scientific definition of a crystal is 'a regular polyhedral form, bounded by smooth faces, and which is assumed by a chemical compound under the action of its interatomic forces, when passing, under suitable conditions, from the state of a liquid or gas to that of a solid'.[1] Clearly, this wants further explanation.

1   *A crystal has to be in a 'regular' geometric form; that is, it has to occur in a form or combination of forms that are in some way out of a geometry text – prisms, pyramids, etc.*

2   *The crystal has to have 'smooth faces'. This really means it has to have 'flat' faces. Irregularities are very common in crystal faces, but they are always repetitions of the flat, smooth faces that are attempting to form.*

3   *It has to be a 'chemical compound', meaning that it has a definite chemical composition, and that for a crystal of any specific mineral, the chemical composition is always the same.*

[1] Edward S. Dana, *Dana's Textbook of Mineralogy*, 4th edn. edited by W.E. Ford (New York: John Wiley, 1982).

4   *The flat faces of the crystal must result from*
     the 'interatomic forces' within it. If we take a
     lump of rose quartz and grind flat faces on it
     in the shape of a quartz crystal (as is often
     done), does it become a crystal? Absolutely
     not, because the faces are not a result of its
     internal forces.

5   *Finally, crystals only form under 'suitable'*
     conditions, when passing from the state of a
     gas or a liquid into a solid. Suitable conditions
     include a hollow space in a rock vein, or in
     a thick magma where the crystals are
     suspended until the whole magma solidifies
     (see Chapter 4). In fact, the majority of
     conditions that create minerals are decidedly
     unsuitable for the formation of crystals.

Minerals and crystals

The word *mineral* also needs to be defined, because crystals are specialized forms of minerals. A mineral is a chemical substance found in nature. A chemist calls SiO_2 silicon dioxide; when it is found in nature, a mineralogist calls SiO_2 *quartz*. To a chemist TiO_2 is titanium dioxide; to a mineralogist it is the mineral *rutile* when found in nature. If the substance is not SiO_2 then it is not quartz; if it is not TiO_2 then it is not rutile. It is some other mineral. When its chemistry changes, it becomes a different mineral. It is therefore clear that a crystal is always a mineral, but that not all minerals are crystals. Crystals are, in fact, a relatively uncommon occurrence of a mineral. (Crystals may also be created and grown in a laboratory. These are discussed later.)

Crystal Forms and Energy

Various parts of the above definition are worked with throughout this book, but the most important part, from the healing standpoint, is the inner nature of the crystal: its perfect inner arrangement, in perfect and harmonious energy balance with itself. To expand the idea of perfect inner arrangement further: a crystal is nothing more than a precisely repeating pattern of atoms. A French mathematician first discovered that there were only 14 different ways of forming regular arrangements of points in three-dimensional space, in 1848. Although Auguste Bravais' arrangements were purely mathematical, they proved prophetic: they are the exact arrangements atoms take when forming crystals. They are, in fact, the *only* patterns possible.

These basic structures into which the components of a crystal arrange themselves are called *unit cells*, a term borrowed from biology. They have also been described as 'electronic bricks' – the final shape of the structure depending on the shape of the 'bricks' used to build it. The overall arrangement of multiples of a cell in three dimensions is called a *lattice*. The crystal lattices are often referred to as Bravais lattices, and all 14 of them are illustrated in Figure 2.

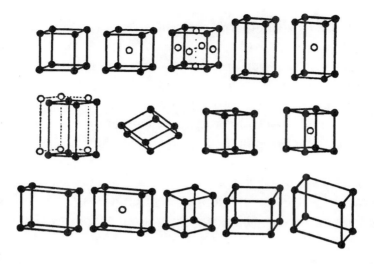

Figure 2: Bravais lattices

Because the inner forces of the crystal that create the effects we utilize as healing tools begins at the atomic, or even sub-atomic level, we need to take a brief look at the atom itself.

Atoms

Atoms are made up of dozens of building blocks, and the smaller the particles become, the more difficult it is to tell them apart from pure energy – indeed, at the smallest level, they *are* pure energy. Matter is just another form of energy. The major components that interact to form crystals are *protons*, *neutrons* and *electrons*. Protons and neutrons are about the same size and weight and make up the central portion of the atom, called the *nucleus*. Protons have a positive electrical charge, and the neutrons are electrically neutral. Electrons are tiny particles with a negative electrical charge, which circle the nucleus at relatively great distances. They like to travel in pairs, and arrange themselves in specific layers (called 'shells')

35

around the nucleus, rather like the layers of an onion. Each shell consists of a specific level of energy; electrons do not move freely from shell to shell, but only when their energy is increased or decreased by a specific amount, called a *quantum* – which is always a multiple of the energy of a photon of light. Electrons can only move from one shell to another; they cannot be 'between' shells, just as you cannot step up half a rung on a ladder.

The shells fill with electrons from the centre outwards, and each shell can only have a maximum of eight electrons. When one layer is full then the next shell fills, and so on until the positive charges of the protons in the nucleus are exactly balanced by the negative charges of the electrons. Unless the protons in the nucleus are a multiple of eight, the outermost shell may not be completely filled – and because the energy shells become weaker the further from the nucleus they are, they can sometimes lose or gain electrons. Moreover, if the number of protons in the nucleus is an odd number, then one of the outermost electrons will be unpaired.

It is these outermost shells of electrons that are of the most interest to us, because it is within these shells that the relationships form between atoms that connect them to one another, and which ultimately create crystals.[2]

Matter comes in three states: solid, liquid and gas. In a gaseous state, the atoms are weakly connected to each other. They are free to move about at random, and are in no particular arrangement. In a liquid the connections between atoms are stronger, but still not strong enough to lock the atoms into a fixed place, although in some liquids

[2] Dr Ronald Bonewitz, with Lilian Verner-Bonds, *New Cosmic Crystals* (London: Thorsons, 2000).

the atoms are relatively inactive, and the liquid is thick enough to behave as a solid. Window glass is such a liquid; very old glass that has been in place for a long period actually shows signs of flowing.

In solid states the atoms are locked into place by the strong attraction of their mutually interacting electrons. When these atoms form very precise and repeating patterns, the matter is said to be *crystalline*; when that inner pattern is repeated in the matter's external form, it becomes a *crystal*.

The mineral quartz illustrates all of these terms. Quartz is a mineral because it occurs in nature, is inorganic, and has a definite chemical composition (one atom of silicon to two atoms of oxygen – SiO_2). The type of the mineral quartz known as rose quartz is 'massive' in form, because it does not usually have flat faces. But it *does* have a regular atomic structure, making it crystalline. The type of the mineral quartz known as *agate* is also a massive form, composed of millions of microscopic crystalline bits, which are not individual crystals. It is cryptocrystalline. It is only when we come to varieties of the mineral quartz such as rock crystal, amethyst, citrine, etc., that we find *crystals*; they are composed of one silicon and two oxygen atoms (SiO_2), they take forms that have a regular atomic structure, and have flat faces arranged in geometric patterns.

Bonding

The 'interatomic forces' mentioned in the definition at the start of this chapter, refer to the way electrons of the atoms of a particular mineral connect to each other in order to form its cells – its repeating patterns. The term for this is *bonding*. There are three basic types of bonding: *metallic*, *ionic* and *covalent*. The *metallic bond* is the simplest and the weakest, allowing the electrons of a metal to move freely from atom to atom, effectively forming a cloud, and holding the nuclei in place in a semi-rigid structure. Metal can therefore be bent and formed without breaking: under stress the electrons are 'herded' around the stress points, leaving the nuclei free to change positions. This is the bond found in crystals of the mineral group called the Native Metals: copper, gold, silver, and so on.

An *ion* is an atom that has either excess electrons or is missing electrons; to balance themselves they are attracted to other ions of the opposite charge, forming an ionic bond.

Ions are created because of the environmental conditions the atoms find themselves in, which add or subtract energy from the atoms. In the Earth these conditions are heat and pressure. In an *ionic bond*, the atoms that are missing electrons link up with the atoms that have excess electrons. It is basically an electrical attraction rather like the attraction between the opposite poles of a magnet. For example, in the mineral halite (rock or table salt), its sodium atoms are missing one electron (giving them a positive charge – Na +), and its chlorine atoms have an excess electron (making them negatively charged – Cl-). The negatively charged chlorine atoms are attracted to the positively charged atoms of sodium. The same thing happens in the mineral fluorite (fluorspar), except that the calcium atoms have two electrons missing (Ca + 2), so each one requires two fluorine atoms to electrically balance the crystal, and give it its chemical formula of CaF_2.

The ionic bond is a strong bond, but because the atoms are bonded in regular layers, the layers themselves are not necessarily well bonded to each other. Ionic crystals are often quite brittle, breaking in flat surfaces in parallel with the atomic layers. The pattern of how a mineral breaks is called its 'cleavage'. How flat and regular cleavage surfaces can be is particularly easy to see in fluorite, which is usually sold in octahedrons cleaved from the irregular cubic crystals in which it is usually found.

The third type of bonding is the *covalent bond*. The number of protons in an atom is usually balanced exactly by the number of electrons, except (as we have seen) in the case of ions. However, electron shells have a maximum of four pairs of electrons in each, and unless the protons are an exact multiple of eight, the outermost electron shell will be unfilled, and some of these electrons, in turn, will be unpaired. The greater the number of electrons needed to fill the shell, the stronger the energy the atom exerts to try to fill its shell and balance itself in all directions. The unpaired electrons or the unbalanced electrons in the unfilled outer shell are referred to as the *valence* electrons; hence *co–*valent. The name also tells us a bit about the bond: the valence electrons are shared between adjoining atoms, so that all of them get a chance to be in balance. The majority of minerals and their crystals have this type of bonding.

Equilibrium and Resonance

The bonding of atoms within crystals has been discussed in a fair amount of detail, because it is crucial to understanding what crystals do, and don't do. And (more importantly), what they *can't* do. Due to the nature of their bonding – the very thing that *makes* them crystals – one of the things crystals *can't* do is 'give off' healing energy. As we can see from their bonding, the forces which tie a crystal together are in perfect balance and harmony – it is what makes a crystal a crystal. A crystal is in a perfect state of equilibrium – that is, it is neither giving off energy nor taking it in. If it were taking in energy, the bonds that make it a crystal would be unnecessary, and it would cease to exist except as a pile of balanced atoms. If a crystal were giving off energy, the bonds would also cease to have any meaning, because its atoms would disappear into a cloud of subatomic particles. Thus crystals *do not* and *cannot* sit there giving off 'healing energy' – it is physically impossible.

But healing does take place in the presence of crystals. So, what happens?

In a word, *resonance*. Resonance occurs when two objects 'vibrate' in harmony with each other. It is a restatement in energy terms of the cosmic law *like attracts like* – like *resonates* with like. Each one of us has our own energy pattern – our soul pattern – that makes us unique. At the same time this energy pattern ties you in a larger sense to all other souls, and all other forms and levels of energy. It is possible to go into the very deepest levels of your own being to experience that pattern directly (an exercise in Chapter 10 will help you do this).

Have you ever wondered why you are attracted to one crystal among hundreds of seemingly identical ones? Like attracts/resonates with like. Your soul pattern recognizes a like pattern in a particular crystal through its resonance with that crystal's pattern. Given that there are only 14 basic crystal patterns, how is this possible? The inner pattern is not all there is to the make-up of an individual crystal. The outer faces are generated by the inner atomic pattern, but the final outer dimensions of the crystals are strictly a product of its growth environment. A crystal an inch long, although having an identical inner and outer pattern, will have a *overall* energy make-up – and resonance – different from a crystal two inches long. Resonance is fundamentally governed by the atomic structure, giving a somewhat similar pattern for each crystal. But the overall physical dimensions, including the development of various faces on the crystal, will change its overall 'character' and make it an unique individual.

If you think about it, this is very much like us. Humans are physically alike in most ways: one of these, two of those, one of that. Our cells are alike, our skeletal structure has the same number of bones in the same position, our soul patterns are very similar, and so on. So what makes us unique? Our total energy make-up. Just like crystals.

This is why, when you pick up a crystal 'cookbook' and it says 'do this' with a particular type of crystal, it often doesn't work. It quite possibly worked for the person who wrote the book (assuming they are a practitioner and not just copying from someone else's book – or 'channelling' crystal uses), so why doesn't it work for you? You aren't that person, and you aren't using their crystals. Even if you did use their crystals – the very crystals they wrote about – it is quite possible that nothing would happen for you. Their crystals would not be attuned to your energy, and your energy relationship – your resonance – with their patients would also certainly be different than theirs. So nothing happens.

In the following pages we look further at the crystals themselves and the forms they take, bearing in mind that it all affects resonance.

External Forms of Crystals

The internal arrangement of atoms based on the 14 basic Bravais lattice cells, yields all of the various external forms crystals take. There are, however, a great many more than 14 external forms. The multitude of crystal forms comes about from the way in which the unit cells are themselves interconnected.

There are some very hard and fast rules that govern these connections between cells. The first and foremost is that cells can only attach themselves to other forms exactly like themselves. At first glance this would seem to suggest an endless repetition of the basic unit cell. But think back to your childhood: many of us had cubic alphabet blocks that could be stacked up in as many different ways as we could think of. Crystals are not quite this free, but in the end the final form will in some way reflect the basic cell of its structure – in this case, the cube. Thus we have a way of classifying crystals by their external forms that also reflects their internal forms: their geometry.

The crystal systems

Crystals whose Bravais lattice unit cells have their geometric properties in common – like cells I – III, based on cubes – are grouped together to form a *Crystal System*. There are fourteen types of cells, and these group into six geometric divisions or systems, which are shown opposite in Table 1.

The first crystal system, based on the simple cubic unit cell (Bravais lattice I), is called the Isometric (from the Latin meaning equal-measure) or Regular or Cubic System. Any crystal of perfect geometric form would fit into a cube with each of its six major geometric points touching the middle of each side of the cube. In nature, we find crystals that are perfect cubes, such as pyrite (Fool's Gold), and halite (table salt). Simple cubic cells can also be stacked another way, to yield an octahedron. Whether simple cubic cells form a cube or an octahedron depends on the geological conditions the crystal

Table 1: The six crystal systems

Crystal System	Bravais Unit Cell	Crystals Forming in the System
Isometric/Cubic	I, II and III	Pyrite (Fool's Gold), Halite (table salt), Gold, Garnet
Tetragonal	IV and V	Zircon, Rutile
Hexagonal	VI, VII, VIII and IX	Quartz, Beryl, Corundum, Calcite
Orthorhombic	X and XI	Barite (Barytes), Sulpher, Topaz
Monoclinic	XII and XIII	Feldspar
Triclinic	XIV	Rhodonite, Albite

forms in, which can shift the energy balance slightly; pyrite can form in octahedrons instead of cubes.

The second crystal system is the Tetragonal System, crystals of which are made from Bravais unit cells IV or V (see Figure 2, p.35). These cells have square bases and rectangular sides, all at right-angles to each other. The next system is the Hexagonal System, made from unit cell VI (with rectangular sides and diamond-shaped bases), or cells VIII or IX (the same diamond-shaped base but with square sides) or cell VII – the shape of a rhombus, but which is still hexagonal when viewed from above. When arranged in a lattice, the diamond-shaped cells create six-sided crystals (such as beryl), and the rhombus-shaped cell creates rhomboidal crystals like quartz.

The fourth crystal system is the Orthorhombic System, which is also known as the Rhombic or the Prismatic System. These crystals are made from unit cells X or XI, which are shaped rather like cereal boxes – the bases and the sides are different sized rectangles, all at right-angles to each other. The fifth system is the Monoclinic System, meaning 'single incline'. Crystals in this system form from unit cells XII or XIII. These are rather like the cereal box-shaped cells of the Orthorhombic System, but they lean in one direction – hence the 'single incline'. The most numerous of all crystals on the Earth, the feldspars, crystallize in this crystal system.

The last crystal system is called the Triclinic System. Crystals in this system have no faces at right-angles to each other. The triclinic unit cell is cell XIV.

Crystal faces

Among the terms the crystal healer will come across while working with crystals is the terminology relating to the actual crystal faces (see Figure 3). A face parallel to the long axis of the crystal is called a *prism* face, and such faces are generally rectangular in appearance. Faces which cut through the long axis are called *pyramid* faces, and they are often triangular in appearance. If pyramid faces are present at several different angles to the long axis, all but the last face may have the points of their triangles 'cut off'. Faces that are perpendicular to the long axis are called *pinacoids*. The combination of faces that makes up the 'point' of a crystal is called the *termination*. If a crystal has 'points' at both ends it is said to be *double terminated*. This last term, in particular, is given undue prominence by some crystal writers, as discussed in Chapter 5.

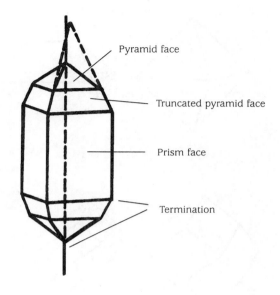

Pyramid face

Truncated pyramid face

Prism face

Termination

Figure 3: Crystal faces

Crystals can occur in *distorted forms*, because of conditions in their growth environment. Sometimes, even though the crystal faces are in the correct position to create ideal geometric shapes, because of the flow of solutions within the vein or locality where they are being created, some faces grow more rapidly than others. This happens, for example, on 'upstream' faces where more new material is encountered in the flow. As a consequence, although all the crystal's faces are in the right place, their relative sizes are out of proportion. A large number of crystals fall into this distorted category. There is absolutely nothing wrong with them – they are just reflecting the conditions where they grew. Figure 4 shows some examples of distorted crystal shapes.

WAY of

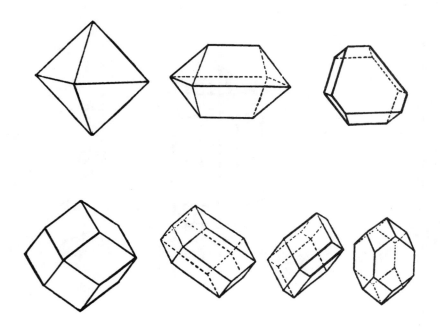

Figure 4: Distorted forms of crystals – octahedrons and dodecahedrons

Postscript

Crystals, like ourselves, are made of atoms, of 'solid' matter. How 'solid' are atoms? Although they behave as if they are solid little balls, they are anything but: if we enlarged the nucleus of an average-sized atom to the size of a golf ball, then all its electrons combined would be smaller than a mote of dust. The outermost electrons would be circling the golf ball in an orbit three miles from it! 'Solid' matter is mostly empty space. If all the empty space was squeezed out of your body, it would occupy far less space than a grain of sand. So, what is 'matter'? Again, mostly empty space: bits of energy in the form of atomic particles held in place by yet more energy. Matter is another form of energy – just as the mystics have been saying for thousands of years. It's *all* energy.

FOUR

HOW CRYSTALS
are Formed

Having seen what makes crystals crystals, and the forms that they take, this chapter will look at the wider environment in which crystals grow, and how changes in this environment create different types of crystals.

The Living Earth

The Gaia Hypothesis states simply that the whole of the Earth itself is a living organism, and all that dwell on or in it, in all of its kingdoms, are part of its life processes. Looking at rocks and minerals by themselves, it is hard to imagine them as being 'alive'. Yet, as with so many things, it is a matter of perspective: what you see depends on where you stand. If you could stand on a single atom and observe the atom next to it, you would see a combination of protons, neutrons and electrons – none of which could be perceived as being 'alive'. But what if this atom is one of those that make up a molecule in the living tissue of your body? Then is it alive? At what point does 'inanimate' matter become alive? What about the mineral matter of your teeth and bones, a calcium fluorophosphate that is the mineral *apatite* when found in the Mineral Kingdom? Is it alive? The way we define 'life' may be in need of rethinking. And, if we stand back from the Earth and observe how it functions in its mineral body – ignoring plants and animals – another picture emerges.

If the Earth is 'alive', then its life processes are driven (at least in its physical body) by internal processes. The central portion of the Earth, called the *core*, is made up of molten minerals, and comprises about a quarter of the Earth's diameter. As the heavy, radioactive elements created in the supernova explosions that destroyed the Sun's ancestors (see Chapter 1) decay, the internal heat of the core

is maintained. Lighter elements such as silicon and oxygen combined with other elements to form new minerals, which were
squeezed outward from the denser core to form most of the rest of
the Earth – the *mantle*. Ongoing heating from radioactive decay
keeps the mantle in a semi-molten, plastic state. The Earth is still
very hot inside, and no matter where you are located, you would
only need to go down a mile or so into the Earth and the temperatures would be hot enough to boil water. Imagine what the temperatures must be like *thousands* of miles down!

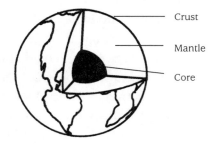

Figure 5: The physical Earth

Floating on top of this flexible mantle, made up mainly of lighter
minerals, is the *crust*. Strangely enough, *floating* seems to be the
exact word that applies. Studies have shown that the crust is very
thin under the ocean basins. At its thickest, beneath the continents,
the crust is just a score or so miles/kilometres thick. At its thinnest,
under the ocean basins, it is only a mile/kilometre or two.

It is the planet's relative flexibility that allows many of its life
processes to take place. The internal structure of the Earth is known
through the study of earthquake waves as they pass through the
flexible earth. Drill holes have only penetrated to a depth of about

five miles (eight kilometres), but there is rock that comes from a much greater depth available for study: that which rises from deep volcanoes, some of which bring up material from the mantle. The Earth's crust appears to be still forming, with new material brought to the surface all the time; it is a major component of the planet's overall functioning as a living entity.

Plate tectonics

The study of continental movement, called plate tectonics (the very foundation of geology), has shown that at one time most of the continents were all part of one supercontinent, which broke apart around the time of the dinosaurs. The most obvious evidence of this is the close fit between the coastlines of South America and Africa. What geologists have discovered is that the crust indeed 'floats' on the mantle, and large chunks of it – the continents – drift about in different directions, sometimes away from each other, and sometimes bumping into each other. Where continents collide mountain ranges are pushed up; where plates are pushed apart, oceans form.

Internal heating of the Earth from radioactive decay causes material from the mantle to rise as it gets hotter, with a corresponding sinking of cooler material, creating large-scale convection currents within the Earth. The convection currents are the propelling forces which bring heated and melted rock to the surface of the crust along fractures in the ocean floors – called rifts – which run parallel to the continental masses. The new material solidifies and is pushed aside by more newly rising material, in turn giving the continents a shove sideways. This happens because the mantle is flexible and the crust is rigid: it is rather like sliding a saucer over a large lump of wobbly gelatine. Some of the heated rock rises under the margins of the continents to create volcanoes.

The surface of the Earth is in constant motion, with much flexing and bending of rock layers: mountains are thrust up, and other layers are bent down and deeply buried. The physical body of the Earth continually renews itself. In the same way, your own body renews itself, reflecting the macrocosm of the planet. The continual cycle of death and renewal of cells means that if you are over 30, for the most part you don't have the same body you were born with – skin renews itself every seven years, and the cells of other organs take greater or lesser amounts of time.

Environments of Crystal Growth

Crystals form as part of the essential life-process of the Earth. On other planets where the organic kingdoms are lacking, the life of the Mineral Kingdom constitutes the *only* life process. The environment in which crystals are created is an essential part of their energetic nature and, ultimately, is reflected in how we interact with them. Crystals are created as part of the rock-forming process. The word *rock* has a very precise scientific definition: a rock is composed of one or more minerals, and is a major component of the Earth's structure. Most rocks are mixtures of two or more minerals, but if a single mineral exists on a large enough scale, it can also form a rock because it is an integral part of the structure of the Earth. An example of this type of rock is limestone, made entirely of the mineral calcite. More typical is the rock granite, composed of at least three minerals: quartz, feldspar and mica.

Rocks (and hence their crystals) form in three basic environments: igneous, metamorphic and sedimentary.

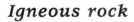

Igneous rock

Most igneous rock originates deep within the Earth and forms from a body of molten rock called *magma*. Magmas may be as liquid as syrup or exist in a plastic state with a consistency and strength similar to that of thick honey. The igneous magma is essentially a very dense solution, with all of the various atomic constituents dissolved in it. The overall composition of the magma determines the minerals which compose the resulting rocks.

Due to the shifting of the continents, zones of weakness and cracks occur in the overlying rocks and molten magma flows upward through these cracks. The magmas may force their way into other existing rocks, or dissolve them altogether, at which point the mineral matter of the dissolved rocks becomes part of the magma. If the body of magma solidifies without reaching the surface, it forms igneous rocks known as *intrusive rocks*, because they have intruded into other rocks. Granite is such a rock. If the magma continues upwards and out onto the surface of the Earth, it becomes a volcano if there is gas in the magma to propel it upward, or it simply floods out onto the surface as a lava flow if there is not. Because they are extruded onto the surface, these rocks are called *extrusive rocks*.

Intrusive rocks cool much more slowly than extrusive rocks, due to the insulating effects of the rocks which surround them. There is much more time for crystals to form – intrusive rocks generally are made of large and well-formed crystals. Extrusive rocks rapidly lose their heat to the atmosphere, solidify quickly, and form only small crystals (generally less than 1mm in length).

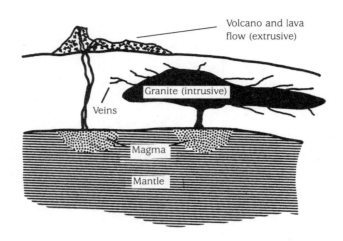

Figure 6: Extrusive and intrusive rocks

The rock basalt has exactly the same chemical composition as granite, but it is an extrusive rock whose crystals have not had time to develop; those crystals that do develop are composed of different minerals than those of granite because of the lower temperature and pressure conditions. We can see from this one example that the crystals we use are created by a complex set of circumstances, that can change through even slight variations in the overall energy balance of the conditions in which they form.

Crystals which form in the main intrusive bodies of rock often do not have the opportunity to express themselves in geometric forms, because as the igneous rocks solidify, the crystals tend to inter-grow with one another. Only when there are hollow spaces within the rock, such as those formed by gas bubbles, that well-formed crystals have an opportunity to develop. As a consequence, an igneous activity that concerns us even more than the formation of large rock-bodies are those crystals that form from the high-temperature, hot water solutions left over when magmas crystallize. Large quantities of liquid and gas charged with mineral matter are given off, which leave the main rock-body behind and make their way toward the surface through cracks in the surrounding rock. These hot-water solutions, usually under great pressure and consequently often reaching temperatures of many hundreds of degrees centigrade, form mineral deposits – and crystals – wherever conditions are favourable. Filled-in cracks or fissures are called *veins* (see Figure 6), and it is from such veins that almost all of our precious metals originate, and many of the other economically important minerals.

There is one type of vein that is of special interest, called a *pegmatite*. The crystals from this type of vein are usually well formed and often quite large. Single crystals from pegmatites have been recorded up to 40 feet (12m) in length, and crystals of 12 inches (30cm) or more are not all that uncommon. Pegmatites are normally associated with the formation of granites, and the basic crystals that form in them are the major minerals of granite: quartz, feldspar and mica. The next stage of crystallization in a pegmatite depends on which metals are present in the hot water solution. If zirconium is present, then zircons form; if beryllium is present, the mineral beryl forms (the blue variety of which is aquamarine, and the green variety, emerald); if fluorine is present, the mineral fluorite may form or, under certain conditions, topaz; if boron is present, tourmaline may form. Or, if various combinations of calcium, magnesium, manganese or iron are present, garnets may form. Equally, it is also possible to find a pegmatite containing only one mineral – usually quartz, although feldspar pegmatites are fairly common in certain areas. It depends on what chemicals are excess to the requirements of the main rock-body.

In pegmatites, crystals always grow to fill the largest space available: if one grows directly opposite another, both will grow diagonally to miss each other. Usually a crystal will grow into the largest open space available to it, even if it has to grow at a considerable angle to the vein wall; some such crystals will grow almost sideways.

A hypothetical pegmatite is shown in Figure 7.

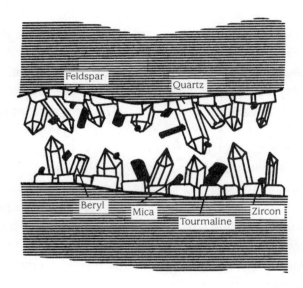

Figure 7: An example of a pegmatite

Other igneous crystals grow from vapour, where mineralized gases escape through vents. These are mainly confined to volcanic regions, and minerals deposited in this way are sulphur, realgar and hematite.

Metamorphic rocks

Metamorphic rocks are those formed when either igneous, sedimentary, or even other metamorphic rocks have undergone physical and chemical changes after their original formation. These changes are the result of deep burial or deformation due to the movement of the continental plates, which bring about temperature and pressure changes, in turn aided by the action of water vapour and other chemical agents. The temperatures and pressures are not enough to melt the rocks to turn them into igneous rocks, but the atoms can still move about enough to add or subtract constituents to the existing minerals, to form new minerals which are more stable under the changed geologic conditions. Minerals characteristically developed during the process of metamorphism are kyanite, staurolite, grossularite garnet (a green garnet) and corundum – sapphire and ruby.

Large-scale metamorphism can cover hundreds of square miles, but there is another type of metamorphic environment called *contact metamorphism*. This occurs when an igneous body has been intruded into the surrounding rock, heating it, and where gases of the igneous body have escaped into the surrounding rocks, causing the recrystallization of these rocks without actually melting them. Where the metamorphosed rock is limestone, there are a number of minerals which can form through the recrystallization of it in combination with mineral constituents of the intruding materials: garnets, spinel, corundum and pyroxene form, along with commercially important minerals such as the ores of zinc and copper, malachite, azurite, smithsonite, sphalerite and turquoise. Less commonly, contact metamorphic deposits may also produce tourmaline, topaz and fluorite.

From the standpoint of the crystal user, metamorphic crystals are next in importance to the crystals formed in igneous rocks.

Sedimentary rock

Sedimentary rock is formed through the processes of wind and water, when the ground-down remnants of other types of rock are consolidated to form new rocks like sandstone and shale. Crystals from sedimentary rocks almost always form from low-temperature water solutions and are usually quite soft (because of the low energies involved in bonding the atoms together). Such crystals can form quite rapidly: in places where crystals are regularly dug out of quicksand deposits – the so-called 'Desert Roses', which are multiple crystals of selenite gypsum – new crystals form within about a year. Halite (rock salt), another common sedimentary mineral, is found in extensive deposits often hundreds of feet thick. But the most common sedimentary mineral is calcite – a calcium carbonate – which forms the rock limestone. It is derived from the shells and skeletons of marine animals living in shallow seas. A commercially important sedimentary mineral is barite (barytes), which forms beautiful blue crystals resembling aquamarine.

'Extraterrestrial' rocks

Mention must be made of what have been marketed as 'extraterrestrial' rocks – tektites. One of the more common varieties of tektites are moldavites, so named because they are found in and around Moldavia. Tektites are irregular blobs of glassy material, varying from green and transparent like the moldavites, to black and opaque, like those found in Thailand. At the time tektites were first discovered, the number of meteor-impact craters known on the Earth was less than half a dozen. In recent years, however, literally hundreds have been recorded, including the huge Reas Crater in Bavaria. Over nine miles (15 km) across, this crater was driven deep into the sandstone underlying the impact area. The chemical composition of the moldavites is exactly the same as the sandstone underlying the crater, and they are found downrange from the impact. Doubt no longer remains that they are melted sandstone splashed out at impact. The crater that produced the Thai tektites has not been identified yet, but there are a number of possibilities. What is certain is that tektites are not 'extraterrestrial'. Any mystical properties attributed to them because of their origins are, perhaps, in the eye of the beholder.

How Crystals are Mined

There are two major types of crystal deposit – *veins*, which we have discussed above, and *placer* deposits. Placer deposits are water or wind-laid deposits comprising the fragments of decomposed veins. Certain types of crystals, particularly those that are harder and more resistant to weathering such as diamond, sapphire, ruby, zircon, garnet, spinel and topaz, also happen to be heavier than the vein minerals in which they form, and often concentrate in beach and stream gravels. Virtually all of the gemstones, except tourmaline and emerald, and at least half of the diamonds produced in the world come from placer deposits. Deposits containing crystals are often discovered by accident, or through the mining of other minerals like gold.

Diamond can be recovered by actually mining and crushing the rock in which it grows, but most crystals are too fragile for this process. Once the diamond-bearing rock has been crushed, it is then mixed with water, and floated across special grease-coated tables. Since

59

water does not stick to the diamonds, they remain perfectly dry and therefore stick to the grease. The other stone, being wet, does not stick to the grease and washes away. The grease bearing the diamonds is then scraped off, boiled away, and nothing but diamond remains. These are then graded and sorted, and the gem-quality stones are sent to the various gem-cutting centres of the world, the most important of which are Amsterdam and Tel Aviv.

Crystals which grow in veins or in pegmatites, are often mined by using nothing more complicated than a hammer and chisel. More complex mining operations, using rock drills, explosives and bull-dozers, are employed in areas that produce sufficient quality and quantity of crystals to make such expensive methods worthwhile. Sometimes it is necessary to follow a vein for many feet before it opens up into a hollow where crystals are able to form perfectly. Such openings are called *vugs* and may contain hundreds of pounds/ kilos of crystals and be several feet across. These are typical of mining in pegmatite areas.

The working of placer deposits is another type of mining altogether. A common method of mining in placers is to sieve or 'pan' the crystal-bearing gravels. By shaking the sieve in a certain pattern under running water, the heavier constituents of the gravel can be easily concentrated at a particular place on the bottom of the sieve, and the crystals that are of interest can simply be picked out. I have used this method to mine sapphire and ruby, topaz and garnet. It is commonly used by small-scale mining operations, often operated by only one or two people. Surprisingly, with the exception of diamond and emerald, the majority of the gem materials available on the market has come from thousands of one or two-man operations.

In larger-scale placer mines, crystal-bearing gravels are run through sluices, which are nothing more than open troughs through which a stream of water flows. Cleats are placed at the bottom of the troughs across the flow of water in order to keep the heavy minerals, which drop to the bottom, from being washed out. The water flow mechanically separates the heavier minerals and washes out the light ones. At the end of the day the trough is emptied and all of the heavy crystals will be caught in the cleats at the bottom. In areas where particularly valuable stones are found these sluices may be dozens of feet in length. This is also a common method of washing for gold.

After the miners have collected their crystals, through whichever method, they are often sold to travelling buyers who move from one small mine to the next. In some countries, such as Colombia, crystal output is controlled by the government, and the buyers are often government agents. The preliminary crystal buyers then sell them on to the international gem buyers, and the crystals are then shipped by the most convenient means possible. If the importer is buying uncut gemstones, he may well carry his purchase away in a briefcase or a coat pocket. If the buyer has purchased large crystals such as Brazilian quartz or amethyst crystals, they are frequently shipped in steel drums weighing several hundred pounds each. It is not unusual for an importer to buy 50 to 100 of these drums at any one time. The importer will then redistribute the crystals he has purchased to various mineral dealers.

Thus the crystal which you purchase may have begun its travels by being washed from a stream or dug from a hillside by a native prospector thousands of miles away, and began its journey to you in a knapsack, or on the back of a burro.

Removing crystals from the Earth

One of the most often asked questions is, is it okay to remove crystals from the Earth; is it harmful to the Earth?

I can only answer that with two personal stories. I had one of the most moving moments of my life when I was digging a quartz crystal out of a vein – not shiny and sparkly like you buy them, but covered with the sticky red mud that had filled in the vein at a later time. As I wiped the mud away, the sun shone through the crystal. And it hit me that this was the first sunlight this crystal had experienced since it was created 45 million years ago. After 45 million years in utter darkness, *I* had brought it into the sun. This is one of my own personal connections to the life processes of the Earth – bringing crystals out into the world from the womb of the Earth.

In my second story, I asked the same question about removing crystals from the Earth, and had the same reservations about doing so. I sat meditating for many hours on the question in a place where I had mined crystals in the past, and it was as if the Mineral Kingdom itself gave me the answer. The words formed in my mind: 'A gift from a lover always has a very special meaning, even if it is only an insignificant thing. As long as you take my gifts and accept them from me in the same state of mind as you accept a gift from a lover, then I am well and truly pleased in the giving of my gift.'

FIVE

FACT AND
Fiction

WAY of

In the previous two chapters I have tried to explain exactly how crystals occur, and what they really are. It is very important to understand the true nature of crystals, because what happens in the healing process is a direct result of their genuine properties. Crystals are always truth embodied, whether their user recognizes it or not, and true healing – finding the inner truth of ourselves – can only take place in the presence of truth. If crystals embody truth, what possible gain can there be in using them falsely? Why not make the small effort required to learn the truth about them, and use them accordingly? Unfortunately over the years many stories and myths have grown up around crystals and their supposed 'magical' powers. These are almost all based on misunderstandings about their genuine properties. As it turns out, what crystals actually do is even better than what they are often believed to do!

One thing that is often misunderstood is that, because energy is the stuff of healing, the laws of the physical universe regarding energy are utterly and completely bound up in the healing process. Because in the purest sense crystals are the laws of physics and chemistry make manifest, there is no way that they can be used to violate the laws of physics and chemistry, nor can they do so themselves. This misunderstanding has led to some of the extraordinary claims made for crystals – things they simply *cannot* do, because to do so would violate these fundamental natural laws, the laws around which the universe and all within it are structured. Even the supreme intelligence of the universe – God – cannot violate these laws, contrary to what is believed in some 'esoteric' circles.

Energy Healing

Energy healing has one huge difference from orthodox medicine: what takes place in its healing processes is often entirely 'invisible'; that is, its actions are unseen by normal sensing or by instrumentation. This is taken by some – especially the scientifically inclined – to mean that nothing is actually happening. Anyone who has worked with energy medicine for any time knows that this is untrue. But equally, it is sometimes difficult to say exactly *what* is happening: an effect may appear to be one thing when it is actually another. What we see – or don't see – in any given situation, is what we have been conditioned to see or, indeed, to not see. This is particularly true of some of the deepest levels of our own being, wherein reside our personal power and, in particular, our ability to heal ourselves and others. These are levels that are often 'invisible' to us, because we have been conditioned not only not to see them, but to believe they don't exist at all. Western culture has usually taken a dim view of people who exercised their energy healing abilities. The consequence is that when we see the results of those powers, we are unable to identify them as belonging to us, and so we need to devise explanations for what we see. These become the myths of crystal healing.

There are several myths about crystals that appear in almost every book on the subject you can find. I will briefly look at some of the more persistent misconceptions (and the reasons behind them), and will then look at those myths that have a more direct bearing on the use of crystals for healing.[1]

---

[1] For a more detailed explanaton of crystal myths, see my companion book *New Cosmic Crystals*.

General Misconceptions about Crystals

Crystals store energy

Crystals are sometimes regarded as a sponge into which vast quantities of electricity can be poured and stored and then squeezed out at some future time for use. This is nonsense. The balance of energies that makes a crystal a crystal makes energy storage utterly impossible. There is no place for it to go. In fact, attempting to pour electricity into a crystal has only one result – the crystal is blown apart from the overloading of its atomic bonds.

This misunderstanding is based upon a genuine property certain crystals have, known as the 'piezoelectric effect' (pronounced 'pie-ay-zoh electric'). This occurs when a crystal is compressed (for example, when it is hit with a hammer). This frees the electrons from the outermost energy shell (see Chapter 3) and releases a flash of visible light and electricity. The effect only lasts as long as the crystal is being compressed, and only until all the available electrons have been released. Once the pressure is released the crystal springs back to its original dimensions, and instantaneously replaces its lost electrons, by either drawing them back from the surface of the crystal, or by drawing free electrons from the air (where there are plenty of them). The net amount of electricity produced is zero.

(This process can also be reversed: rather than compress the crystal to give off electricity, we can put electricity into the crystal to cause momentary expansion of the structure. This causes the crystal to vibrate – a property which is widely exploited in, for example, quartz watches and tourmaline torpedo contact detonators. At no point is energy being stored in the crystal.)

Quartz myths

There are many, many misconceptions about quartz, mainly due to its usefulness in the modern electronics industry. Quartz resonators are used in radio transmitters, in receivers and in amplifiers, but they are *not* amplifiers or transmitters. In fact they are only a small part of the electronics of the transmitter or amplifier, and are used solely to control their frequencies (through the same piezoelectric properties described above). Some writers on crystals seem to believe that you only have to stick a crystal in your ear and dial Peru, or that Egyptian priests sent one another radio messages on quartz crystals!

Nor does quartz (or any other crystal) store light – for the same reason that crystals cannot store electricity; nor do naturally occurring crystals convert light into electricity. These misunderstandings arise because of the confusion surrounding the terminology relating to quartz and its components. Light conversion occurs in the artificially grown crystals of silicon *metal*, which do not occur in nature.

Another misconception is that quartz is used in computers: there is *no* quartz used in computers. It is the crystals of artificially grown silicon *metal* (the so-called 'silicon chips') which are used in computers. The confusion arises from three similar-sounding words: silic**a**, sili**con** and silic**ate**. Quartz is the mineral name for the chemical silicon dioxide – silic**a**; sili**con** is a metal, as noted; and a silic**ate** is a member of a group of several hundred minerals containing silic**a** as one of their components. Quartz itself does not even belong to the silic**ates**, because it is an oxide of the metal sili**con**, and therefore belongs to the mineral group the Oxides.

Perhaps the myth about quartz being 'special' derives in part from the mistaken (and often repeated) belief that it is the most abundant mineral in the Earth. The most abundant mineral is olivine, an iron – magnesium silicate. Its gemstone variety is peridot. The mantle (which makes up two-thirds of the mass of the Earth) is, in fact, mostly olivine. Quartz is not even the most abundant mineral in the crust of the Earth – there are hundreds of times more feldspar in the crust than quartz.

Quartz does, however, have the greatest number of *varieties*. Mineralogists divide the varieties of quartz into two separate types – *vitreous* (meaning that each of the varieties has a glassy appearance), and *cryptocrystalline*, meaning that it is made up of microscopic quartz crystals. The vitreous varieties include rock crystal, amethyst, smoky quartz (properly called morion), citrine and rose quartz. The cryptocrystalline varieties include agate, jasper, flint, chrysoprase, sard, sardonyx, carnelian and many others. However, other minerals, such as garnet, also have large numbers of varieties.

Let us remember when we try to set quartz apart from other minerals: there are 2,500 different minerals – quartz is only one of them.

Other misconceptions

'Crystal'

There is a tremendous amount of confusion about the word 'crystal', because the word is also applied to a type of glass. 'Glass' is a very specific scientific term, with a very precise meaning: it is a liquid that is so solid it will not flow at ordinary temperatures. The characteristic of a liquid is that it's totally structureless – its atoms are arranged in no patterns whatever – making it completely opposite to natural crystal. Making colourless glass was very difficult, and the process wasn't perfected until about AD 1500. If you had anything made from 'crystal' before that time, it was made from quartz. After 1500, glass that was as colourless as natural crystal was called 'crystal glass' to differentiate it from ordinary glass. The properties of natural crystals are a direct result of their structures. Structureless 'crystal glass' has none of the properties of natural crystal – which doesn't mean that it can't be enjoyed for its own beauty.

Liquid crystals

Liquid crystals are similarly of little immediate importance to the crystal user, in that they are semi-solids in which the molecules of the liquid arrange themselves in regular patterns when electricity is applied. It is thought that much of the memory-storing capacity of the brain is made up of liquid crystals. Liquid crystals are generally microscopic in size and, although of great importance generally, are of little use specifically in crystal healing.

External forms of crystals

Much emphasis is given to the external forms of crystals by some. There is certainly a relationship between the shape of a crystal and static electricity, since static electricity accumulates on the points and edges of crystals. Unfortunately for those who make interpretations based on this, static electricity also accumulates on the points and edges of everything else! Whether it is the point of a pencil, the tip of a cat's tail, the peak of a house or the tip of your nose, there will be a static electricity accumulation.

Given this emphasis on shape, we might expect to carve the shape of quartz crystals out of blocks of wood, and presume that they would behave exactly as natural crystals. Obviously they do not. When lumps of a mineral like rose quartz are cut into the shape of crystals – as almost all rose quartz 'crystals' offered for sale have been – their new external shape has no effect on their crystalline properties. They might as well just stay lumps.

Striations

Striations are parallel lines running across the prism faces of quartz crystals, which some people have decided are like the bar-codes on packaging. Apparently these are meant to be messages from the past encoded onto quartz crystals by the ancients before they buried them hundreds of feet underground through solid rock, somehow fusing them to the walls of veins. Leaving that aside, striations are natural features created in the crystallization process from the pull of forces within the crystal as temperatures and pressures within the vein vary. Given one set of conditions the crystal produces prism faces, but if there are slight changes in conditions, rhombohedral faces start to form the crystal's 'point'. The striations are nothing more than rhombohedron faces that haven't been completed – there is no mystery about them whatsoever.

Birthstones

The whole idea of 'birthstones' was cooked up by the Victorian jewellery industry to sell those gemstones that were in abundance at that particular time. A look at the lists of birthstones produced will reveal that there are almost as many different lists as birthstones, and it just so happens that the stones appearing on the lists at any given time are those stones that happened to be abundant then.

Male and female crystals

The origin of this idea comes out of Native American mythology and was originally connected to turquoise. Mother Earth is represented by green, the colour of growing things, and Father Sky is, naturally enough, blue. Turquoise was particularly prized, and it comes in both green and blue shades; green turquoise was regarded as 'feminine' or Mother Earth turquoise, and blue turquoise as 'masculine' or Father Sky turquoise. If we ourselves embody a great deal of feminine energy we might well experience crystals reflecting back our own feminine energy back to us, but it doesn't mean that the crystal itself is female.

The term 'feminine' eventually became applied to milky, cloudy quartz crystals. Crystal miners in most of the places where quartz is produced had mountains of milky crystals that they couldn't sell because everyone wanted the clear ones. They couldn't give the cloudy crystals away. Conveniently, the milky crystals suddenly became 'female' and their market value rocketed!

This doesn't mean that the milky crystals aren't – and weren't – of value. They are still crystals, and therefore still perfect. All that has changed is our perception of them. Nonsensical terms like 'male crystals' and 'female crystals' are not needed to justify what is and has always been.

Other terminology

Like other practices, crystal healing has developed its own language. While different writers use terms like 'rainbow crystals', or 'wands', or 'dolphin crystals', these are more often than not the creation of a few crystal users and, aside from having no genuine crystal meaning, are far from universal. The creation of many of these terms is an attempt by their creators to make themselves 'special', by indicating that they have a supposed knowledge that is unique to them.

Misconceptions About Healing with Crystals

Crystals emit 'healing energy'

This myth is addressed elsewhere in the text, but to summarize: the thing which makes a crystal a crystal is its perfect energy balance. Where is this 'healing energy' supposed to come from? If a crystal emits energy, it has to change, to shrink or become something else. The only crystals that 'give off' energy of any kind are crystals of radioactive minerals. They emit radioactivity, but in the process they decay and change into something else.

The other point constantly missed is this: we live on a planet *made* from crystals or crystalline material. If all of this mass of mineral matter is continually sending out healing vibrations, how on earth could disease even exist?

Perfection

A common myth is that crystals have to be 'perfect' in order to be useful. 'Perfect' is usually taken to mean that they have to be transparent, with no chips on them, and that they have grown in an undistorted form. What makes crystals do what they do is their atomic structure, their inner pattern, their inner nature, not their external form.

Crystals can be cloudy, chipped, battered and beaten, but they are still perfectly usable for healing purposes, because their inner nature is unchanged. If a crystal wasn't 'perfect' it wouldn't be a crystal in the first place – perfection, like beauty, is in the eye of the beholder!

Double termination

The word 'termination' just means the point on a crystal: the end of the crystal. In some quartz crystals (in fact you'll find it on all kinds of other crystals as well but, once again, people tend to focus on quartz), there is a point at both ends – it is *double terminated*. The idea is that double-terminated crystals develop both ends at the same time and are therefore something special, with special healing powers.

However, it is actually more prosaic than this. Double-terminated quartz crystals form when the crystal breaks off from the cavity in which it is forming, and it just grows another point on the broken end. There is no big mystery about it at all.

Synthetic crystals

Several different types of crystals are grown artificially, and most take on the same forms and mundane energy characteristics of their natural counterparts. Quartz crystals are grown for the electronics industry, ruby crystals for lasers, sapphires for bearings and substitute gems, emeralds for gems, diamonds for industrial use, silicon carbide as an abrasive, and rutile, cubic zirconia and garnet as diamond substitutes. In the latter cases, the variety of garnet grown is yttrium-aluminium garnet, which does not occur in nature, nor does cubic zirconia, and silicon carbide forms lattice-like, iridescent black crystals, which are beautiful but which do not occur in nature.

Crystals grown that are not found naturally must inevitably violate the laws of natural matter; they have, in a sense, been 'forced' to grow against their own nature. Obviously, crystals grown in such environments are not likely to harmonize well with natural energies. However, the aspect of all synthetics that makes them generally unusable for healing purposes is that, at a subtle level, crystals embody the energy of their growth environment. The growth environment of an artificial crystal is clinical, sterile and far removed from any sort of natural environment.

Specific crystals heal specific diseases

The idea that one type of crystal can heal a particular disease is a complete myth. First, a great many diseases are not just a single 'malfunction' of a single organ or body part, but are a complex mix of interacting deficiencies. For any given patient, some deficiencies will be more prominent than others, but in every instance the disease, in its overall makeup and effect, will be different for every patient. For example, we tend to speak of 'cancer' as a single disease, yet in its orthodox treatment, there are over 70 different chemotherapy drugs alone that can be used.

Second, many 'diseases' that have a physical component are themselves manifestations of deeper problems, which are often non-physical in nature. To use the example of cancer again, it has been found that personality types categorized as 'rigid' have a much greater tendency to develop cancers than other, easier-going types.

Third, as we explore further in Chapter 6, the interaction between a given healer and a given patient is in many ways unique. Since this interaction, at the level of real healing, is purely energetic, a crystal placed into the energy interaction may resonate in one way in one set of circumstances, and in an entirely different way in another. One crystal healer in Holland has over ten thousand recorded cases of crystal healing, and has found that, for him, certain crystals tend to help in specific circumstances. But when other people use the same crystals – literally the same crystals in some cases – *nothing happens*. This is because another person using those crystals will, at a subtle level, have a different energy relationship with the patient.

Finally, as noted in Chapter 1, many 'crystal-healing' books draw on other crystal-healing books, which in turn drew originally on old and even ancient material on healing. We can find 'healing' with crystals mentioned by Pliny the Elder – in about AD 70 – and in even earlier Egyptian sources. The main problem with old sources is that we cannot be sure of either what disease they were referring to, or what crystal. The names of diseases have changed over the centuries, as have the names of minerals. For example, 'sapphire' in Pliny's time referred to any blue stone, and his references to 'sapphire' may, in fact, refer to lapis lazuli. But, there is no way to be sure. Additionally, much of ancient medical practice was based on treating 'like with like'; in other words, if the ailment or injury produced a blue colour in the patient, it was treated with blue medication: flowers, minerals or foods.

It is worth repeating: by all means try the ideas suggested in crystal books, but let your own sensitivities and the responses of your patients – or your own response if you are self-healing – be your guide. Truth is not something that is experienced in your head; it is an internal body sense, a 'feels right' feeling, and it is the only sure way to heal, with crystals or otherwise.

SIX

THE CRYSTAL
Mirror

As many crystal users have discovered, many of the claims made about crystals simply don't work in real life. Crystals possess no mysterious properties: like all else in our world, they simply reflect. They are mirrors. What they mirror back to us are the same levels of energy they embody – those levels that are perfectly balanced, harmonious, and in perfect arrangement. Thus crystals mirror back to us the portions of ourselves we tend to be the most out-of-touch with – the portions wherein reside our own personal power: our ability to heal, our ability to create wholeness; the portions we mistakenly believe belong to the crystal when we see our reflection in it.

Mirroring is the basis of the old truism, *like attracts like*. That truism can be expanded further: in order to attract like, like must first of all *recognize* like. How does it do this? Because, in some respect, like must also *reflect* like. Just as the reflection in a mirror, if there were no reflection, there would be nothing to recognize. In an earlier chapter, the word *resonance* was used to describe the process through which the human organism responds to crystals. Resonance, reflection and mirroring are all words for the same process. Thus we can also expand the truism to include: like *resonates* with like. But what, exactly, resonates?

Some years ago I was involved in an experiment which used a biofeedback device called the Mind Mirror. It is essentially a EEG for reading brainwaves, but with the various levels of brainwave activity displayed in rows of lights on a panel, divided into left and right brain hemispheres, making the patterns of the various levels simultaneously visible. The test subject was blindfolded and wore earplugs to eliminate as many outside distractions as possible, and entered a meditative state. When the brainwaves stabilized, crystals taped to the end of a meter stick – to minimize the amount of the experimenter's aura getting involved – were passed through all of the chakra points.[1] The subject was unaware consciously of the point at which the crystals passed through the aura. As the crystals passed through the lower three chakras – the most earth-connected chakras – there was a strong flare of brainwave activity in the subconscious levels: the body was instinctively aware of their presence. The experimenter's conclusion was that this was the 'recognition' mechanism at work: like very clearly resonating with and recognizing like.

Mirroring the Divine Essence

Many spiritual sources teach us that we are in a new stage of evolution even now, with the coming of this New Age of the Earth – the Aquarian Age. But we are also being taught that this is an evolution in consciousness, and it will be the pattern of evolved consciousness that new lifeforms will take.

It is significant, then, that at a time when men and women are becoming resensitized to the world around them, the very earliest energies of the universe are the last ones we have become sensitive to. We have tended to think of the energies of minerals as the lowest form of energy, but seen from the standpoint of the evolution of the universe, the Mineral Kingdom formed under the *highest* energy conditions and therefore, in a sense, represents the *highest* energy to which man can attune. For these energies carry the very imprint of the creation of the universe, and having chosen to live in a world of crystalline matter, we therefore align ourselves with the same creative impulse, the so-called 'Thought in the mind of God' that is the motivation of the universe.

[1] Chakras relate to different levels of energy in auras, and are explored further in Chapter 10.

Thus do we not have this same aspect of creativity that is our very spiritual nature, our own 'divine spark'? Do we not have this same ability to visualize, to see in our mind's eye, some object and then go out and build it? Is this perhaps what we mean when we say that man is made in the image of God? Herein lies the key to the very existence of the race of man: we *are* a part of the Divine Essence that *is* creation; we are here on the Earth to participate in that creation. Man is a synthesis of matter and spirit within himself – a being of spirit bearing a body of matter – which is a perfect microcosm of the universe itself: the Divine Being whose body is the physical universe. This synthesis is vital to the evolution not only of man but also of the Earth itself.

Why? What is it we are here to do?

Think back for a moment to the beginning of the book. The universe is still mostly made of hydrogen, the lightest and simplest element. Look at the sky tonight, and what do you see? Thousands of stars – and beyond them there are thousands and thousands of millions of stars that cannot be seen. All doing one thing – taking hydrogen and making heavier elements out of it. The universe is getting *denser.* The whole pattern of evolution of the universe itself is from lighter matter to denser matter. And as the physical universe becomes denser, doesn't the level of energy we call spirit also need to begin to inhabit that denser matter? And isn't that exactly what we, as beings of spirit, are learning to do on the Earth?

We have been thinking of ourselves and the Earth as some kind of a spiritual backwater: many of us see ourselves encumbered with these awful dense bodies that we have to drag around, and we look forward to the time when we can slough them off for good. It has been useful to believe this, but the truth is finally dawning for many:

what we are really here to do is exactly the opposite: to regain our enlightenment as a spiritual race, and begin what we were created to do; to learn, not how to escape from matter, but how to live fully and richly – to fully embody life – while still living as dense matter.

The Plant and Animal Kingdoms are doing the same at their own levels of consciousness. How closely linked the Human Kingdom is with those Kingdoms, both in our mutual embodiment of dense matter, and of how closely that matter is related within all the organic kingdoms, is being revealed through the science of genetics. For example, humans and trees have about 70 percent of their DNA in common; chimpanzees and humans share all but 1 percent of the same DNA. And, ultimately, we all share the same source of the building blocks of life itself: the Mineral Kingdom. We are *all*, in a sense, evolved minerals.

So, what is the reality of crystals? In the simplest terms, they are tools to which the deepest inner part of ourselves responds, in a clear and potent way. It happens whether we are even aware of it or not, whether we know anything about crystals or not, or whether or not we attach any spiritual meaning to the process. But however we view the process, it is we who are doing the responding, not the crystals. The crystals, like the mirror on the wall, just sit there, being what they are. There is no need for mystical mumbo-jumbo. The truth is not only 'out there'; it is simplicity itself.

The interactions that create mirroring

The actual mechanism of mirroring has to do with the human energy field, often called the aura, and its interaction – its resonance – with the crystal. Ted Andrews lists the following four characteristics of the aura that are directly involved in the mirroring process:

1   *Every person's aura has its own unique
     frequency*. No two auras are entirely alike.
     There may be similarities, but each is an
     energy field unique unto itself. When the
     frequency of your aura is close to that of
     another, there is a natural rapport. Where
     another's aura is greatly different from yours,
     there may be an instant dislike for that
     person, or feelings of discomfort, agitation,
     etc. It doesn't necessarily imply that there is
     something wrong with the other person;
     rather, the two energy fields are not in
     resonance with each other.

2   *Your own aura will interact with the
     auric fields of others*. Every time you come
     into contact with another person, an
     exchange of energy can occur. The more
     people you interact with, the greater
     the energy exchange.

3   *The human energy field – the aura – can
     interact with animal, plant, mineral and
     other energy fields*. All matter has energy
     fields because of its atomic structure,
     although the fields of animate matter are
     stronger and more easily detected. There is
     a lot of truth to the healthy habit of hugging
     a tree, which have dynamic energy fields
     that interact dynamically with human
     energy fields.

4   ***The longer and more involved the contact, the greater the energy exchange**. Your own aura leaves its imprint upon that with which you interact, which can be another person, a part of the environment or even an inanimate object. The longer and closer the contact, the stronger the imprint will be: your aura charges the environment with an energy pattern in harmony with your own. The basis of psychometry (reading the vibrations from objects) is a direct result of the interaction of the individual's aura with that object, in that the longer the person has had contact with an object, the stronger it becomes charged with an energy pattern that is similar to that of the person.*[2]

Let's look at Andrews' four points in order, to see how they affect mirroring.

Every person's aura has its own unique frequency

Not only does every person's aura have its own unique attributes, so do the auras of all other forms of matter, both animate and inanimate. Each crystal is itself a unique entity, and although their inner patterns are identical, their final forms will all be different in some way. Like snowflakes, no two crystals are exactly the same, therefore their mirroring will be slightly different; they will interact with identical energy fields in slightly different ways. Even for the same crystal, because no two people are exactly identical energetically, its

[2] Andrews, pp.12–18.

mirroring will thus be different. For one person it mirrors one thing, but for another person the same crystal will mirror something else. So, when the energy fields of each crystal and each person are both different, it is clear that the chances of one crystal or type of crystal being the same for everyone are virtually non-existent. This demonstrates clearly the nonsense that specific crystals have specific uses.

Your own aura will interact with the auric fields of others

This is the most crucial point of the interaction between the healer and the patient. Because their energy field is in some way different from yours, and from every other person's you will encounter, when exactly the same crystal is brought into the healing interaction, there is no reason to expect that anothers' response to it will be the same as yours. Not only that, no person's aura – or yours – is likely to be exactly the same from one encounter to the next – so what you did last time and what crystal or crystals you used may well not apply in the new energy relationship. As you can see, trying to work all of this out in your mind is virtually an impossibility. That is why the healer needs to train him or herself to respond to their own 'feels right' feelings in the healing situation, and why the idea that specific crystals heal specific illnesses is a nonsense.

The human energy field – the aura – can interact with animal, plant, mineral and other energy fields

These properties of the aura are the specific properties that create mirroring. Your energy field interacts with the energy field of the crystal, and you sense your field's response. But with crystals, there is not just *any* response. The mirror on the wall can only show you the state of your physical being. It can't show you your mental, emotional or spiritual state (except through the interpretations you make, based on your own physical appearance). Thus the nature of the material from which the mirror is made confines its reflections to a certain level. So it is true with the crystal. But as shown earlier, the inner nature of the crystal is such that it reflects very deep levels of your being, wherein resides the very essence of who you are. And, by contrast, those parts of yourself that are not in harmony with that essence. This is why you are attracted to certain crystals and not to others – some part of you resonates with some aspect of the crystal. This is also why, in Chapter 8, so much emphasis is given to choosing crystals, and why it is recommended that you always choose them for yourself. Because it is part of you that is interacting when you feel drawn to a specific crystal, no one else can or will ever have that same interaction. Thus no one 'knows' more about what is right for you than you do.

All this doesn't mean that every crystal you use or are drawn to will always invoke 'feel good' feelings. Some of the inner issues that need to be resolved will definitely involve 'feel *bad*' feelings: this is where you need to focus on the 'feels *right*' feeling, regardless of any other responses you might have. It is an important dimension of personal growth and development to be able to distinguish between the two.

The longer and more involved the contact, the greater the energy exchange

Andrews' word to describe the contact was 'intimate', but he was relating it more to human relationships than with inanimate minerals. However, exactly the principle applies. Intimacy implies a deep level of connection, which can happen quickly or over time through prolonged contact and connection. It is through this process that certain crystals become 'yours'.

Specific crystals for specific ailments

Throughout the book emphasis has been on the uniqueness of each person and each crystal, in an effort to demolish the myth that specific crystals are used for specific ailments. From the above paragraphs, we can begin to understand exactly why this is so. A workshop experiment clearly demonstrates the reality and exposes the myth. How people genuinely respond to crystals is clearly demonstrated time after time in an experiment performed hundreds of time in courses, with the same result every time, without fail. It is one you can do yourself. It is best to have ten or more people, but it can be done with less, keeping in mind that the less people involved, the narrower the set of possible responses.

Seat the participants in a circle with their eyes closed. Ask them to keep their eyes closed throughout, and to hold out their right hand. Have them keep their hands flat, so they cannot sense either the size or shape of the crystal; in other words, eliminate as few physical clues as possible, to keep the thinking mind as disengaged as possible. Going around the circle, place a crystal in each open hand. After a few minutes, ask the group what they are experiencing with the crystal. Out of a group of twenty, three or four will experience sensations of heat; another three or four will have sensations of cold. For a few it will feel very heavy, and for another few it will feel very light; others will feel as if it is getting larger, and some will feel as if it has disappeared altogether. Some will see colours or other visual experiences, or have sensations in other parts of the body. Within the group many will have exact opposite experiences, and others will have highly varied experiences. But the secret is, until they open their eyes, they will not know that you have given them all the *same* type of crystal – all quartz, all amethyst, all topaz, or whatever. This exercise can be done as many times and with as

many types of crystals as you wish; the result is always the same –
a number of opposite reactions, and a wide range of other responses,
although not necessarily from the same people who had a particular
reaction the last time.

There is another experiment you can do that demonstrates how and
what a crystal mirrors depends on where it is placed. This can be
done alone or with others, but when there are several people
involved, there is a wider variety of responses. Once again the participants hold their right hand open and flat, but this time their eyes
are open and they place the crystal themselves. First it is placed in
the centre of the hand, and the reaction sensed; then it is moved to
the tips of the fingers, and the reaction sensed in that position; then
it is moved to the heel of the hand, and then to the wrist, again sensing as before. This one small demonstration shows that an inch or
so in the placement of a crystal changes our response to it, clearly
demonstrating that our own energy field varies even over a small
distance. Thus which crystal you will be drawn to will be in some
way affected by where and how you are intending to use it.

Different teachers say that in use, the crystal's termination should
point in this direction or that direction. As the above experiment
demonstrates, and in the experience of the writer with many workshop groups, there is no particular rule about this except that there
will be a certain way that some crystals will feel natural in the hand,
that the crystal will naturally point. But, that direction varies greatly
from person to person, so go by whatever feels right to you. Try it
for yourself: lay the crystal in your open hand and rotate it through
a full circle. There will be a certain point where it just feels *right*.
It is this *right* feeling you are looking for whenever you work with
crystals.

Where and how the crystals are placed or held has been the subject of a great many crystal books. Varied placements and patterns are suggested. In some they are laid out along the body at distances believed to correspond to different levels of the aura. Others are laid directly on the body over the chakra points. Others are held by the healer and moved in patterns across the body. There is nothing fundamentally wrong with any of these, except when they are done because they *must* be done in some specified circumstance. Every single person involved in every single treatment – 'patient' or healer – is a different person every single time. Energetically we change from second to second, thus *every* 'healing' is in some manner different from the last. We need to understand that the patient–healer interaction needs to be one of sensitivity to the needs of the individual patient, and not the repetition of a formula from a book. Energy healing differs from allopathic medicine in precisely this way.

So what about the uses of crystals listed in the various crystal books? By all means *try* the uses suggested, but be sensitive to the response and the result. What works for one person may have no result at all for another trying exactly the same thing: it is the nature of energy healing, and of mirroring.

We should remind ourselves again of the bottom line: it's *all* energy – energy arranged in different patterns. Your own life is about energy patterns: patterns of growth and development; patterns of relationships; patterns of *relating*, to yourself and to others. Finally there is our own deepest inner pattern: the soul pattern if you like. Energy patterns are, ultimately, the patterns of creation itself, and of which man and minerals are both a reflection.

SEVEN

COLOURED
Crystals

Colour and its effects in the healing process are the most neglected properties of crystals. In most books on 'crystal healing' there is inevitably a list of illnesses and a list of crystals that are supposed to heal them. But what is rarely noticed is that a very large portion of these healing effects are due to the *colour* healing properties of those crystals. Colour is one of the most important ways that crystals perfectly balance their own internal energies. Colour is a result of internal interchanges of energy, including sunlight.

Colour and the Body

Colour healing comes from and is an important segment of the realm of energy healing. The relationship of the physical body to colour, and how colour can be used to keep the body in a state of harmony and balance – health – has been the work of many colour therapists and serious medical researchers for centuries. In 1903, for example, Danish physician Niels Finsen was awarded the Nobel Prize for Medicine for his work on light and colour in healing disease, and around the same time, physician Dr Dinshah P. Ghadiale successfully began healing with different coloured lights, a process now known as chromotherapy.

As explained in Chapter 2, a person's psychological state is part of the whole-body state that affects overall health. Colour psychology has been the study of numerous eminent psychologists and psychiatrists, such as psychoneurologist Dr Kurt Goldstein, a founder of Humanistic Psychology. His studies of colour and its effects underscored the work of Drs Ghadiale and Finsen, as well as colour therapists and other colour researchers: not only do colours affect the entire human organism, and that each colour has a role to play, but that a good balance of colour was necessary for a healthy life. **89**

Goldstein's studies confirmed that colour-response is deep-set, intimately entwined with the entire life process, and that various mental conditions and psychological states have definite and varying responses to colour. Later researchers have confirmed his work, including Dr Robert Ross of Stanford University, who found that certain colours are allied to dramatic intensity and strong emotion, and Dr Maria Rickers-Ovsiankina who confirmed even earlier work with the colour preferences of introverts and extroverts.

Colour has measurable effects on our sense of the passage of time, sense of space, of taste and of smell. In turn, it has been shown to be affected by various sounds. Clearly, our entire organism is reactive to colour and, quite clearly, the colour of the crystal or crystals we use must therefore have a profound effect on the healing process. Indeed, as noted in Chapter 1, it was because of their colour that crystals were first used for healing.

Light and Colour

Light is a small portion of the electromagnetic spectrum, which includes X-rays, radio and television waves, microwaves, ultraviolet and infrared light, and many other waves, waves that are the characteristic movement of these types of energy. The distance between the crests of the waves determines which type of wave they are: television and radio waves have wave-crests a metre or more apart, whereas at the other end of the spectrum gamma rays and cosmic rays have crests only billionths of a metre apart. More or less in the middle of the spectrum is the tiny portion of electromagnetic waves we see as visible light.

Within this portion of the spectrum are further gradations of wave spacing – colours. Here, the widest wave-spacings are at the red end of the spectrum, with the narrowest at the purple. The other colours fall in between, with the order of their spacing following the colours of the rainbow. Just off the visible spectrum at either end are infrared and ultraviolet light, invisible to us but visible to other creatures such as snakes and bees. When we consider how narrow the spectrum segment of visible light is, and how many colours the human eye can determine within it, we begin to see how incredibly important colour is to our existence.

All of us know that light is essential for life, but what is it that makes *colour* so special? Quite simply, on our planet, life – including human life – evolved within the narrow range of the spectrum to which we are sensitive. Like microwaves on the longer side of the spectrum and X-rays on the shorter side, a considerable portion of the electromagnetic spectrum is actually fatal to life, especially human life. Our atmosphere screens out harmful radiations; in fact, any lifeform that was likely to be affected by those radiations would never have evolved here in the first place. Thus the very evolution of the human body is intimately keyed to colour, as the scientific findings from the researchers noted above have demonstrated. When we interact with coloured crystals, we are interacting with the very stuff of life, at many levels.

Colour in Crystals

As we saw, the arrangement of atoms in unit cells is determined by two things: size, and electrical potential. Occasionally an atom will slip into the crystal's structure as it forms that is *nearly* the same size and electrical potential as the rest of the atoms making up the

91

crystal – but not quite. Because the crystal structure exists specifically for the purpose of creating perfect balance, it averages out and balances the effects of the foreign atoms by absorbing light and/or electricity. The light that is absorbed by the structure restores the balance, but only certain wavelengths are absorbed to redress that imbalance. The 'unused' wavelengths are not absorbed – and it is these that determine the colour of the crystal. Such is the exquisite balance within the crystal that it takes very few – as few as three or four foreign atoms per million – to cause colour. The technical name for the 'foreign' atoms is *trace elements*.

The trace element causes a deformation of the lattice (see Chapter 3), and the electrons of the surrounding atoms shift to compensate. Sometimes the atomic lattice is deformed for other reasons, such as a shift in the growth conditions during crystal formation. Even without a trace element present, this deformation of the lattice can 'trap' an extra electron, creating an energy imbalance to be counterbalanced by light absorption in corresponding wavelengths. Precisely how the rogue electron 'traps' energy is unknown: one professor of physics remarked that this question belongs more to the realm of philosophy than physics!

The amount of trace atoms that it takes to cause coloration is tiny – only a few atoms out of every million normal ones. How little it takes can be easily imagined by visualizing a cube of quartz with sides of 12 inches (30cms), and realizing that the amount of iron that it would take to turn that cube into amethyst is less than the amount of iron in the head of a pin.

In synthetic materials, trace elements are often deliberately added to change the properties of the base material. For example, the silicon chips that are used in computers (regularly confused with quartz in crystal books!) are silicon metal (which is electrically unresponsive) to which a small amount of a trace element has been added, usually phosphorus, giving the chips their electrical properties. So, not only is quartz not used in computers, even the silicon metal has to be tampered with to get it to do anything. Neither silicon metal or its alloys occur in nature.

Gemstones are often heat-treated to change their colour, and within the last decade certain gems such as diamonds have had their colours changed by irradiation with X-rays. In both of these treatments, when foreign atoms are present there is a change of energy state in these atoms, freeing extra electrons to absorb different wavelengths of light. An example of this is brown zircon, which is regularly heat-treated to turn it blue. There are also certain varieties of amethyst that can be heat-treated to turn them yellow-brown (citrine). In quartz, where an occasional aluminium atom has substituted for a silicon atom, if this crystal has grown in an area where there is no natural radioactivity in the rocks, the crystal will remain colourless. However, if it is subjected to even a relatively small amount of natural radiation, the crystal will assume a range of colours from yellow-brown to black (citrine and smoky quartz). Much of the smoky quartz on the market has been artificially irradiated to produce its colour.

Mechanical deformation of the lattice

As an example of how the presence of foreign atoms in the mineral structure causes colour, we will look at corundum (Al_2O_3) – a fairly boring name as mineral names go. But where the occasional atoms of chromium have substituted in the structure for an atom of aluminium (chromium and aluminium atoms are approximately the same size), the entrapped electrons then absorb the energy of

93

certain wavelengths of light to rebalance the structure. The only wavelength that 'escapes' is red, thus producing a corundum that is 'coloured' red – the variety called ruby.

The titanium atom is just slightly larger than the aluminium atom, and it also fits into the corundum structure – rather like putting a size 6 foot into a size 5½ shoe: it will fit, but it pinches! The 'pinch' in this case is a disturbance of the energy bond surrounding the titanium atom, causing a slight distortion in the crystal lattice. This is a different level of energy distortion than that which chromium atoms produce, thus the wavelengths absorbed to balance it out are different. Here, the colour that escapes is blue, creating blue corundum – the variety called sapphire. Therefore sapphire and ruby are exactly the same mineral, but are different colours because of a different trace element.

This is true not only of corundum, which has dozens of distinct colours because of differing and varied amounts of trace elements, but of other minerals as well. A common example is fluorite, which also comes in dozens of different colours. However, because fluorite has no particular value depending on its colour, there has never been a need to give each colour a different name.

Rubies are almost always smaller than sapphires because chromium, even in minute percentages, causes a disruption in crystal growth and inhibits the growth of crystals. The presence of chromium automatically ensures that the crystal it is colouring will be smaller than it would have been otherwise: there are very few large rubies known in the world.

So, does chromium always cause a red colour? As a matter of fact, it doesn't. It isn't the chromium *per se* that causes the red colour, it is the distortion it produces in the lattice. Put exactly the same chromium atom in a different structure, and it will produce a different distortion; therefore the colours absorbed to create balance may well be different. This is illustrated by the mineral beryl: when there is a trace of chromium in its structure, the colour escaping is green, creating the variety of beryl called emerald.

Using Coloured Crystals

When it comes to the use of coloured crystals in the healing process, how is one to know which to use? Every crystal will be somewhat different from others of the same type, varying in colour and trace-element make-up. There are two answers to this. First, the intuitive approach suggested previously and, second, find a good book on colour therapy, such as those written by English colour expert Lilian Verner-Bonds.[1] In choosing and interpreting a crystal colour, Verner-Bonds makes the following points:

1   *There is no perfect stone for everyone: all crystals have their own worth, and their own messages and experiences to be encountered.*

2   *Colour is also a medium to learn to exchange and interact with: like crystals, there are no good or bad colours, only information to be gained. The key factor is how you interact with your coloured crystal, the value of which is personal to you.*

[1] The colour psychology and healing material that follows is based on Lilian Verner-Bonds' chapter, Chapter 8, in *New Cosmic Crystals*.

3   Each stone, whether you are comfortable with
     it or not, gives you insights.

4   If you wish to reflect aspects connected to
     your intuitive, physic ability then use your left
     hand when choosing a coloured crystal; this is
     known as the side leading to divine power,
     directly through the heart.

5   For more mundane information relating to
     your life on a day-to-day basis, use your right
     hand. If you cannot decide which to choose,
     you can close your eyes when selecting and
     you will, on a certain level, still be choosing
     the coloured crystal that pertains to you and
     your situation.

6   When you have chosen, check the following
     paragraphs for the understandings that that
     particular crystal colour has given you.

7   When you concentrate on the colour of the
     stone you are holding, does it feel strong
     or weak? Sit quietly and experience any
     sensations. You may just have sensations
     in your hand, or your mood could change.
     Perhaps all of your senses are involved.
     Whatever happens, you will be shown
     something you need to know.

8   If the feelings you experience are
     uncomfortable ones, use the colour you have
     chosen to pinpoint why.

9   *If you seem to experience nothing at all, regard the colour of the stone as being perfectly balanced within your system at that moment.*

The Psychology and Healing of Colour

Below are described a number of colours, and their shades, tints and combinations, in terms of their psychological and personality meanings, which are also the meanings of the colours themselves. When working with a coloured crystal and you wish to focus on its colour dimension, read its colour characteristic as either personality or colour appropriate to how you are using it at any particular point. With the characteristics of each colour are listed crystals that are found in that colour, some of which may appear under several colours, since that is how they occur. Where a mineral variety takes its name from its colour, like citrine in quartz, or emerald and aquamarine in beryl, the variety name will be listed. This chapter deals with the seven basic spectrum colours, although Verner-Bonds' work covers extensively other colours such as white and black, and (uniquely among colour therapists) the brilliance – the transparent, crystal clear light from whence all colours ultimately spring.

Shades and tints

All tones of a colour share that colour's basic qualities, but they are modified by whether they are shades or tints.

Tints are pale colours, and have more white in them than the pure hue. Because of the energy-boost given them by the white, they are stronger for healing purposes. It also makes the personalities that embody them much lighter than those embodying the pure hue. Pale pink is more powerful for healing than the basic hue of red for example, because of the abundance of white in it. Since white has an equal amount of all the colours of the spectrum, any tint has its basic hue supplemented by yet more of itself within white. White always strives towards a purity of spirit, and is a great opener that allows expansion and creativity. It is a great overall cleanser. Thus crystals that are white or are tints are, from a colour standpoint, good basic colour healers.

Shades are the basic hue mixed with black, and are darker. Although tints are usually considered positive and shades negative, the negative can be just as useful, in that it directs us and tells us what we need to look at. Black is a colour rejected by some therapists but it is, in fact, related to life's deep mysteries, visionary ability and the mystic secrets. Not all that many centuries ago black was considered to be God's own colour. Black is safe and hidden, and allows a 'stand still' period to occur. Thus if you are drawn to coloured crystals that are shades, or are even black, you may be putting certain personal issues on hold, seeking a deeper illumination of them, or both.

The colours and their characteristics

Below are listed the specturm colours, their characteristics and the chakras (body energy-centres that relate to the aura) they relate to. Chakras and chakra healing are discussed at length in Chapter 10.

Red – Root Chakra

Red is the great energizer of the spectrum, and promotes courage and the will to overcome. Within the body, red is connected to the circulatory system. In healing, it is often used for irregularities connected to blood, the arteries and general circulation. It is a powerful stimulant, so it should always be used in moderation.

Shades of red can reflect a tendency to become overaggressive, quarrelsome and to act before thinking things through.

Tints of red – the pinks – reflect universal love, kindness and affection. Those drawn to pink tend to be easy going and forgiving, but they can be oversensitive.

Red Crystals: Ruby – Garnet – Tourmaline – Rutile – Cinnabar – Rhodachrosite – Spinel

Pink Crystals: Diamond – Tourmaline – Morganite – Garnet – Dolomite – Rhodonite

Orange – Sacral Chakra

Orange is the colour of assimilation. It represents our ability to absorb the goodness from life, focusing on the physical necessities of life. It not only helps break down barriers, it is a colour for putting things together again when all seems lost. It is a colour for healing hidden phobias, shock symptoms, bereavement and grief. Physically, it is useful for kidney complaints, torn ligaments, broken bones and the relief of menopausal symptoms.

Those drawn to the shades of orange feel thwarted, that life has let them down. The peach tint of orange works on a gentler level than the major hue.

Orange Crystals: Dark Citrine – Zircon – Realgar – Calcite – Vanadinite – Wulfenite – Garnet – Spinel – Topaz – Orthoclase

Peach Crystals: Peach Beryl – Topaz – Calcite

Yellow – Solar Plexus Chakra

Yellow is the colour of mental and intellectual stimulation. Those who relate to yellow are great ideas people, full of vision and originality, with the ability to communicate. It is a great cleanser, releasing toxins from the body, relieving constipation and digestive disorders, and healing disorders of the skin and nervous system. It is an uplifting colour, excellent for depression and weariness of the spirit. Gold embodies wisdom accumulated from experience, and knows how to put action into motion because of the knowledge it has of mankind. This is the colour representing forgiveness, but without denying self-worth. As a healer, it helps all chronic skin complaints, can be beneficial for stimulating an under-active thyroid, and is successful with depression.

Those connecting to shades of yellow can be tense, sarcastic, nagging, evasive, lazy and inefficient. The pale yellow tint reveals those who are practical, fair and reliable. They have a mental agility and are broad-minded, enabling them to cut through baffling complexity.
Yellow Crystals: Diamond – Citrine – Apatite – Sulphur – Brazilianite – Sapphire – Scheelite
Light Yellow Crystals: Citrine – Topaz – Spodumene – Scheelite – Topaz
Gold Crystals: Gold – Pyrite – Marcasite – Topaz – Barite

Green – Heart Chakra

Green is the balancer, the middle colour in the rainbow. The aim of green is harmony, with the ability to see both sides of a story. Green heals pains of the heart, and affairs of the heart emotionally; it is the great healer and balancer. It is a good general detoxifier, stabilizes bleeding, and helps centre oneself in times of physiological illness.

The shades of green can reveal hypochondriacs and emotional dictators. Dark green at its worst represents greediness or the miser. But there are two sides to dark green; it also exposes those who have an inclination to always do things at the expense of themselves. Pale green tints represent fresh starts and new beginnings, as it reflects back youth's hope and inspiration: people drawn to pale green tints can be both idealists and, at the same time, very practical.

Those who relate to turquoise are extremely cool and very balanced, but with a fire burning underneath. Turquoise tells you it's about time to jump off the fence and get on with it. Turquoise reminds you to think of yourself first for a change, instead of always fixing it for everyone else. It is good colour for healing the emotions and pains of the heart, and helpful for minor skin rashes and problems, and for light fevers and infections.

Green Crystals: Emerald – Malachite – Dioptase – Apatite – Sapphire – Epidote – Olivine – Zircon – Jade

Light Green Crystals: Jade – Garnet – Smithsonite – Prenite – Amazonite

Turquoise Crystals: Turquoise – Smithsonite – Aquamarine

Blue – Throat Chakra

Blue begins the energetic movement away from the physical body toward the more spiritual aspects of life. Honesty is a key attribute of blue; it is the colour of truth. Blue represents a need for self understanding and emotional understanding. Blue slows the metabolism, and is a mild-to-medium painkiller. It is beneficial for arthritis and rheumatism, and in the relief of stomach ulcers. Children's ailments such as teething, ear infections, sore throats and fevers respond well to blue.

Shades of blue can indicate reclusiveness, or someone stuck in a rut. There may also be a tendency to meanness of spirit and deceitfulness. But it can also show that life's experiences have been learnt the hard way. The pale blue tint inspires and uplifts the spirits, giving support and encouragement to release one's self from constraint and restriction, and also to understand that which cannot be changed.

Blue Crystals: Sapphire – Sodalite – Lapis Lazuli – Spinel – Zircon – Kyanite

Pale Blue Crystals: Diamond – Barite – Turquoise – Celestite – Topaz

Indigo – Brow Chakra

Indigo is about structure: duty will be the core of motivation of those who relate to indigo. The indigo of the sky and oceans hold the secrets of the great unknown, beckoning you to step into the threshold of the mysterious. There is an all-or-nothingness to personalities who connect to indigo: they never have an in-between, yet they always comes up trumps. Chest, bronchial or lung complications, migraines, varicose veins, boils, diarrhoea, swellings and sinus problems all respond to indigo. The strongest painkilling colour of the spectrum, indigo is best used for adults, and should only be used in extreme cases for children.

Indigo does not appear as a tint, but as a shade it can reveal a very moody temperament. There may be a leaning to spiritual fanaticism – not listening to anyone else's opinions. They have no respect for their bodies, and have a tendency towards an addictive personality.

Indigo Crystals: Sapphire – Kyanite – Azurite

Purple – Crown Chakra

Purple corresponds to the highest elements of man's nature: gentleness and power. But combining the two is the challenge. Musicians, poets and painters – those with the highest creative gifts – can be found here. It is the colour of leaders and masters, who are often the loners who march to the beat of a different drum. Purple's main province is the brain, making it the healer of all conditions relating to that organ. It relaxes the muscles, including the heart. It is a good colour to slow down over-active kidneys. Purple releases menstrual pain, decreases bleeding and haemorrhaging, and provides support for the eyes, neuralgia and general inflammations of the nervous system. Lavender is a great aid for the person who seeks to delve into their psychic ability.

When purple becomes a shade, there is a tendency to pompousness, spiritual social climbing, delusions of grandeur and an inability to recognize the true spiritual path. The lavender tint reveals a light disposition and a buoyant temperament. Yet they see with vision beyond the physical eye, possessing a deep understanding of destiny for themselves and others. They are much stronger in mind, body and soul than they first appear.

Purple and Lavender Crystals: Amethyst – Sugilite – Apatite – Lepidolite

EIGHT

GETTING
Started

Despite the enormous complexity of the interactions that take place when crystals are brought into the healing process, their actual use is simplicity itself, and involves only a few, distinct stages.

Acquiring Crystals

The first of these stages is to acquire your crystals. It is enjoyable to find your own crystals whenever possible, and not all that difficult. Aside from pleasure of collecting, there is the added benefit of the extra closeness with the Earth itself. Not all areas are blessed with good collecting localities, although it is often surprising what is available in your own neighbourhood. You can find out by making enquiries at your local museum, through geological societies, or even the geology or earth-science departments of a nearby university. You may also be able to find guide books written for the collector, and often available through mineral dealers, that describe various collecting localities. If you happen to live in or near a city with a bookstore dealing in textbooks of various sorts, you may very well find some interesting guide books tucked away in areas of the shop dealing with geology and mineralogy. Some of these books or periodicals (like the *Lapidary Journal* in the USA) will also carry advertisements for places where you can go to collect crystals on a fee-paying basis. Thèse are sites where crystals are already being found, and your chances of finding crystals in such places are very good.

In a number of countries, there are clubs for people who collect rocks and minerals, who will have knowledge of and access to many good collecting locations. Enquire about such clubs through mineral dealers, or try the local telephone directory. These clubs are very popular in Australia, New Zealand and the USA.

If you are fortunate enough to live in or near an area where mining or quarrying has taken place, there are excellent possibilities for finding crystals in the waste rock from both types of operations. Always be certain you have permission from the landowner or mine operator to collect, and be aware that these types of locations can be extremely hazardous. Under no circumstances should you enter mine tunnels or underground workings, as they are often quite unstable, and cave-ins and rockfalls can happen quite easily. Also be quite cautious when walking in such areas, as vertical shafts will often be overgrown and difficult to see until it is too late. If you take children into such areas, keep them in sight (and within easy reach) at all times.

Whenever you are in the countryside where rocks are exposed, look out for any changes in their appearance, especially changes in coloration that appear as straight lines or streaks. Often these will be veins of a different mineral, and can contain crystals. Beaches and stream beds are also good places to find all sorts of rocks and minerals, although they are much more likely to be water-rounded. This does not necessarily detract from their usefulness, and once again your own sensitivity and awareness will tell you which crystals want to come home with you. If you have been drawn to this book, you may already have piles of rocks and crystals on every available shelf!

The most common method of acquiring crystals is to buy them. There is certainly nothing wrong with buying crystals, since you are exchanging the energy you have put into acquiring your money for the energy that the crystal has 'accumulated' in making its way to you, maintaining the balance of energy that characterizes a crystal. A crystal 'acquires' the energy of the miner, of the buyer, the importer and of the cost of transportation required to reach the mineral seller.

Most 'New Age' shops sell crystals, and your local telephone directory is also good a place to begin your search. Depending on the part of the world in which you live there will be several types of headings to look under. These may include 'Rock Shops', 'Minerals for Collectors', 'Lapidary Equipment and Supplies', or 'Mineralogists'. Many of the businesses listed under these categories will not have crystals available for sale, but they may well know where you can enquire further in your local area.

Choosing a crystal

Crystals can often be purchased by post, but it is best to make your own choice in person. It is sometimes tempting to have someone else choose a crystal for us, someone who supposedly 'knows' more than we do about them. *Always* choose for yourself; anyone who chooses for you has taken away the opportunity for you to expand your own awareness and intuition. Many methods are suggested for choosing crystals: dowsing with bent coat hangers, muscle testing through kinesiology, etc. There is really nothing wrong with any of these methods, but in choosing a crystal you are really looking for one that resonates in some way with your Inner Being. If you are choosing a crystal to reflect the healing aspect of yourself, then one particular crystal above others may resonate, whereas if you are choosing one for meditation, a different crystal will resonate.

How you actually decide between crystals is simple. Only choose what you are drawn to – 'drawn to' being the sense of attraction to a specific crystal that comes from your resonance with it. Forget that you are a Leo or a Sagittarius, or that some book or other says you should have such and such a stone. You are a unique individual, just as each crystal is a unique individual. This uniqueness is part of the subtle make-up of both you and the crystal, and the only way that uniqueness can match up is through the inner sense that says: 'This feels right.' Many people believe that they are not very intuitive, but almost every one of us has had an experience of a 'first impression' – something inside us that tells us there is something about a person or place that either does or does not tally with what we are told. Later events invariably prove the 'first impression' to have been correct! This is really nothing more than a flash of intuition.

For those who do not have confidence in their intuitive ability, what might be called the 'first impression method' is suggested. It is very easy – just stand in front of a number of crystals, shut your eyes, relax, and then open your eyes quickly and grab the first crystal that your eye is drawn to! In that instant, before the thinking mind can react, your intuition (which is instantaneous) has already flashed to the right one.

If you are choosing crystals for a specific purpose such as healing, then have this purpose in mind, or even project it to the crystals, and see which one responds; that is, which one you are drawn to. Some people actually sense an energy response from a particular crystal – almost as if the crystal is jumping up and down saying 'Me! – Me! – Me!' Whatever the response or the attraction to a particular crystal, it is a crystal that is in some way like you – a perfect out-working of the universal law of 'like attracts like'.

You may be asked, or feel drawn, to choose a crystal for someone else. There is nothing wrong with this, as long as you again choose intuitively. A good method is to visualize the person for whom you are choosing the crystal, project that visualization to the crystals, and see which one responds.

Occasionally you may be drawn to a crystal without knowing why. It may be that if that crystal is for you, it is for some time in the future. This may be the only chance you and the crystal have to get together: when the crystal is finally needed it may not be possible to be physically present in the same place. Alternatively, the crystal may be for someone else, perhaps someone you have not even met yet, and you have the opportunity to acquire the crystal that they may not have. Again, the intuition takes care of these situations. If you are given a crystal, or are not sure why a particular crystal has been drawn to you (or you to it), meditation may provide the answer. This is discussed in Chapter 10.

Keeping crystals

Many users feel that personal crystals, i.e., crystals that are used solely by one person, are best kept out of sight and not handled by others. This is so that the large amount of personal energy involved with such a crystal is not disrupted. It feels appropriate in many instances to keep these crystals in a dark place – such as in bags made of black, blue or purple velvet – when not in use. Crystals for self-healing will certainly fall into this category.

You may sense that where others' energies are involved, crystals in general use (such as healing crystals used in a practice) can be on display and be handled by anyone. Again, your individual intuition will tell you how your crystals should be kept.

Some crystals are 'happy' with certain other crystals, and not so happy with others. This has to do with the resonance of their natural energies. Thus you will sense that some crystals will harmonize next to one another on a shelf, and some will not. In either case, it is no reflection on the inner qualities of the crystals involved.

When using your crystals there will probably be one direction or another that the crystal will naturally point. Different teachers say that the termination point should face in this or that direction. In the experience of the writer with many workshop groups, there is no particular rule about this, except that there will be a certain way that some crystals will feel natural in the hand. As that varies greatly from person to person, go by whatever feels right to you.

Basic Crystal Use

Once you have selected your crystal through whatever process, there are several stages that are suggested in putting it to use. As you read various crystal books, you will find there are nearly as many techniques as there are books. In truth, it doesn't matter what activity you undertake in any of these processes. As in all things in the world, it is solely a result of your intention and not the activity itself that is creating the response. As the term *mirroring* is used throughout, it will be helpful to look at the various stages of crystal use in these terms.

Cleansing

The first stage is *cleansing*. If crystals are mirrors of the Self, then cleansing is nothing more than cleaning the mirror! Physical mirrors get fingerprints on them, they get cloudy, they get dusty – in other words they need to be cleaned so you can see a clear reflection. Crystals as mirrors are exactly the same: what they are mirroring is energy, and therefore the reflections they give are energetic in nature. Likewise, that which keeps a crystal from giving a clear reflection is also energetic, and therefore the 'cleaning' of a crystal also takes place at an energetic level.

Since crystals are used primarily in dealing with subtle energies, and since these energies tend to have an effect on the very nature of the matter that makes up the crystals, it will be necessary to cleanse them occasionally of any undesired energy. It must be made clear that the crystal is not 'storing' this energy but, rather, that the existing energies of the crystal have undergone some subtle change within themselves. Through the crystal's contact with the Human Kingdom, there is some sort of energetic shift that takes place within it, a change of consciousness, a change in the *nature* of the energy it embodies.

These are the sort of subtle changes that take place in inanimate matter that can be picked up through psychometry. In crystals, these changes can come about as a result of being dug from the earth originally, from being handled by the miner, from the various crystal dealers who have sold and resold it, or other people who have handled it or whose thoughts and intentions have been impressed upon it. The act of cleaning, then, is nothing more than returning the crystal's reflectivity to the required state. There is a parallel within your own experience: you still have exactly the same number and arrangement of atoms in your body before a profoundly enlightening experience, but afterward you are definitely changed.

In the process of cleansing a newly acquired crystal we want to leave in all the natural energies and take out any of the energies it has accumulated since that time. Remembering that crystals respond to the intention of the user, it is enough just to intend that these natural energies remain, and they will. What to do with energies that you have deliberately placed in the crystal and wish to retain, is discussed below.

The actual technique of cleansing varies from individual to individual, and you will find a technique through experimentation that will be right for you. You can just wash your crystals in flowing water, the universal cleanser. You may be familiar with the effect of salt water in cleansing your own body's aura, and a similar effect is seen on the 'aura' of a crystal. A word of caution, though – do not use hot water on your crystals, as it is likely to shatter them. Always use water that feels cool to the touch, or cold water – the water temperature should match the temperature feel of the crystal as nearly as possible. Hold the crystal in your hand while washing it, and intend that all consciousness impressed on the crystal, and not desired, be washed away; and that all desirable consciousness it has absorbed will remain.

Sunlight is also always a great cleanser, so leave your crystals in the sunlight, with the intention of cleansing any undesired energies. Allow your own sensitivities to be the judge of the necessary time. Do be aware that some of the intensely coloured crystals will fade if exposed to sunlight for long periods. Some people suggest washing crystals in eucalyptus oil or surgical spirit (medical alcohol), or breathing on them in a certain manner. Truly, it does not matter: in each instance, it is the *intention* of the user to clean the crystal that is important, and it is this intention to which the crystal responds. In actuality, any method or technique you use is just a physical reinforcement of your intention.

My personal method for cleansing crystals is to use a simple visualization, as all that is really necessary to clean a crystal is a focused intention. My personal symbol of purity is clear mountain spring water, so I just visualize a flow of that water through the crystal, washing away anything that I don't want in it. With an 'unprogrammed' crystal, I visualize the water washing away anything that was not part of the original nature of the crystal; with a 'programmed' crystal (see below), I intend for it to retain its original nature plus whatever programme I have imprinted in it.

The question of when to clean crystals apart from the initial cleansing will largely depend on the intuition of the user, as well as on the use to which they are put. Crystals that are being intensively used and which connect with a number of different people – such as those used by a healer on a regular daily basis – will need frequent cleansing, perhaps even between each patient.

Programming

Programming is the act of choosing the reflection you wish to have come back to you from the crystal. When we programme a crystal for healing, we are really tuning ourselves to the reflection back to us of our own ability and capacity to balance and harmonize. Used in a clinical situation, a crystal reflects to the patient their own natural abilities for self-healing. It is *our* intention that is creating the action, and the crystal is acting purely as a reflector. If you programme a crystal for meditation, then you are selecting a reflection back to you of some higher aspect of yourself.

There will be a certain amount of subtle energy already 'programmed' into your crystal that is a result of the natural environment in which it grew. This may not be apparent in its physical form, but with experience of discerning energies you will be able to tell a piece of quartz crystal that has come from Arkansas in the USA from a Brazilian one. In the former you will find a very clear and crisp energy; in the latter a much more diffuse and less intense energy. In choosing your crystal, your intuitive response will automatically acknowledge differences in the original growing environment, and you will always choose the crystal that grew in the environment necessary to harmonize with your own particular energy. Remember also that in choosing a crystal for a specific purpose such as healing, you have already chosen a crystal that is to a large degree in harmony with its intended use. Thus programming is a reinforcement of the original intent.

You won't need to programme all of your crystals in advance, especially those carried for personal use whenever a need should arise: just programme them as you use them. Crystals that are used for a single purpose, such as healing or meditation, benefit most from conscious programming, where it is particularly desired that the crystal should retain its programme.

The actual process of programming is simple: just direct a thought into the particular crystal, intending that that crystal's energies should be focused for a particular purpose, and that the crystal should retain that particular thought or intention within itself. During this process it is most effective for the crystal to be held in the hand, to help the crystal harmonize totally with the energies of your aura. All of this will be imprinted in the crystal during the process of programming. Other books suggest various programming methods – select one that feels 'right', and follow it, remembering that all 'methods' do is to reinforce your intent.

It is also possible to programme into your crystal a 'self-cleaning' programme, whereby the crystal will automatically clean itself as you use it. Once again, a little experimentation on the part of the individual user will determine the best method.

Protection/Consecration

Another stage related to programming may be called *protection* or *consecration*, which is, once again, nothing more than being selective about the reflections. In this case, it is reflections which we *don't* wish the crystal to give. My personal protective programme is that I don't wish a crystal to reflect anything that is not in harmony with what I call the Christ energy. There are a lot of energies around in the world, energies at many different levels of life and different levels of being, but the Christ energy is an energy that applies solely to the human race, and all other energies in the world are in harmony with it. It is the highest level of energy within each of us, to which all other energies of our lives are directed, whatever name we call it. If we think about it for a minute, the only inharmonious energies in the world are those created by humanity.

The question naturally arises that if crystals reflect perfect balance and harmony, how can they reflect back that which is not perfectly balanced and in harmony? The analogy with your bathroom mirror is apt: when you look in the mirror, does it not reflect back everything? But when some of the things it reflects are not as they should be, do we not know *because of* the reflection that something is not right? So, too, is it with crystals: when they reflect back something that is out of balance, the nature of the reflection calls our attention to the fact that we have to take action to bring ourselves back into harmony with the Christ energy.

All of these steps can be performed with a single thought, but in the beginning it helps to break things down into stages. Those of you who are using crystals already are undoubtedly familiar with these steps, and have perhaps developed your own variations on them.

It is always best to programme crystals yourself. There are plenty of 'experts' around who will offer to do it for you, but your deepest Inner Being always knows best what is right for you. What all of us are ultimately working towards in this life is taking full responsibility for ourselves and for our own lives, and this is another small way in which you can begin to do that. So what if you make a mistake? There is no way you can harm yourself with crystals anyway.

Crystals and Personal Development

Our work with crystals goes hand-in-hand with our own spiritual awakening – the process of gradually integrating our total spectrum of personal energy from the densest and most material, to the highest and most spiritual. As you progress from point to point in this awakening process, your own total energy make-up, or auric resonance, undergoes a change.

As you become more and more aware and awake spiritually, and as your own particular resonance changes, different crystals come into your life to correspond and harmonize with those resonances. A crystal is an expression of universal consciousness and that, as a particular crystal (which is also part of that universal consciousness), begins to correspond and harmonize with our particular energy, we can find through the crystal a gateway to our own process of realization, a point of contact with the Universal Mind.

It is also true that a particular crystal which was 'ours' at a particular time of our life may not be so in the future. Therefore, we should look on crystals as spiritual tools, and not as possessions. When our work with a particular tool is finished, we can lay it down and go onto the next appropriate tool. We do not discard the tool, but rather pass it on to someone else who needs it. You can be certain that when you are finished with a particular crystal in your life, the Universal Consciousness will make absolutely certain that the next person who needs that tool will be drawn to you. It is then up to you to recognize this fact and pass the crystal on in an appropriate manner to the person who needs it. There is certainly nothing wrong with selling it, if this feels appropriate. The pattern of the universe involves exchange of energy, and money is a valid form of energy exchange. On the other hand, it may feel totally inappropriate. By the time you have developed your sensitivity sufficiently to know that you are finished with a particular crystal, you will also have the sensitivity to know the appropriate method of transferring it to its next user.

NINE

CRYSTAL
Therapies

This chapter is written both for the person who wishes to become a crystal healer and the person undergoing crystal healing, as an indication of what to expect when receiving treatment. Chapter 10 contains exercises and illustrations relevant to the material of this chapter.

The most important single consideration when either giving or receiving crystal-healing therapy is that it should generally be treated as a *complementary* therapy, not an *alternative* therapy – *especially* when the patient is undergoing regular medical treatment. No reputable complementary practitioner will *ever* recommend the suspension of orthodox treatment, or propose complementary treatment in place of prescribed medication. It is perfectly acceptable to use complementary treatments to subdue the side-effects of medication however.

In energy medicine the relationship between the healer and the patient takes on a greater degree of importance than in other treatments; it is a fundamental part of the energy-healing interaction. Research into other related areas such as psychotherapy have consistently shown that the results of therapy are better where an empathetic relationship exists, and where the patient and healer have a comfortable and easy interaction. In general, it has been found that, from the patient's viewpoint, the therapist is even more important than the particular therapy undertaken. This is an equally important factor in crystal healing. If seeking treatment, choose a therapist with whom you are comfortable, and in whom you feel confidence. The actual treatment given may vary from healer to healer, but if you feel comfortable and confident with them, the form of the therapy will likely be the right one for you.

No one ever goes to a therapist unless there is a problem, and some anxiety is natural. But, if you have any doubts or reservations – don't undergo treatment with that person. A reputable therapist will usually offer to meet with you beforehand if there are likely to be a number of sessions involved, and if it is a preliminary session and you aren't happy, reputable therapists will not have a problem with this. If they do, you are in the wrong place anyway.

Likewise, as a crystal healer you will find some patients with whom you just don't connect, or who don't connect with you. To attempt to continue a healing relationship in these circumstances is unethical. It is important to realize beforehand that there will always be some people who will not feel you are right for them, and it is not a judgement on you or your healing ability.

Along the same lines, reputable practitioners will have a code of practice, and you are entirely within your rights as a patient to ask about it in detail, as well as to ask about the practitioner's qualifications, experience and healing results. It is true that many crystal healers will have no formal qualifications, as there are none which exist in the same sense as orthodox medical qualifications; but a general query about experience and results is entirely in order. Again, any therapist that has a problem about these types of questions should be avoided.

Having just said that medical-equivalent qualifications don't exist, there are a number of schools of crystal healing in various parts of the world that offer training courses and issue diplomas. In a few countries such as the UK, associations of healing schools exist and, again, qualifications are offered at that level. But remember, for the most part the operators of the schools do not have formal medical training, and the diplomas and qualifications issued by them operate under that limitation. It doesn't mean that the crystal healers they train are not potentially good healers; it just means that the pieces of paper on their walls may reflect considerable variations in quality. The cautions about the choice of healers in the above paragraphs applies here equally. Reputable schools and associations should be willing to provide you with a written code of practice, and some type of written information about the certifications they offer, and what they mean.

General Approaches to Healing

There are several types of healing which take place in a healer-patient relationship. The most commonly used is *contact healing,* where the healer places his hands directly within the aura of the person, or often directly touches their physical body. Crystal healing is often performed as contact healing; that is, where the crystal (or crystals) are placed directly into the energy of the subtle bodies. The healer diagnoses the area of energy disturbance, and places the appropriate crystal into that area. The crystal can be selected either by the patient or by the healer; the sensitive healer will be aware of which option is correct for the particular case. The crystal can then be held by the healer, or by the patient, or perhaps even worn by the patient for a short period of time. Again, the correct method will suggest itself. Some common sense is necessary here for therapists, though. You are not likely to win converts for crystal healing if you have patients walking around for two weeks with a crystal tied to their head by a piece of purple ribbon, as one over-enthusiastic crystal healer did – especially when, as in this case, the patient was a burly truck driver! In any case, the crystal serves as a focus of healing energy and healing intent, and mirrors the patient's own healing potential.

Other treatments involve the patient lying on a couch or treatment table, and the healer lays a complex pattern of crystals around the patient, or even, in some cases, on the patient. There are numerous courses and books which teach these patterns, and, as long as they are used through the intuition of the healer and are not just rigidly applied as if they *must* be done, they are perfectly acceptable.

Another method is for both the patient and healer to hold crystals, although obviously the two crystals need to be in harmony with each other. One osteopath uses crystals that have been sawn in two: the patient and the healer then hold separate halves of the same crystal. An alternative to this method is for the patient, or the patient and the healer, to hold crystals of different minerals in different hands. There is often a reflective interaction between the crystals of various minerals and a balancing effect may be produced through the natural energies of the differing crystals. The actual minerals used will vary from patient to patient and can only be sensed by the healer, or by the reactions of the patient.

Internal organs

In the treatment of the internal organs, we cannot implant a crystal into the organ, or have direct access to it, other than access to the diseased organ's reflection in the disturbance of the body's energy field. Australian Aborigines do actually implant crystals into patients, but usually only under the skin. In most cases of healing diseased organs, the crystal is held or placed into the area of disturbed energy on the outside of the body; as the energy field reharmonizes, so does the diseased organ. There is no specific rule as to the exact distance the crystal is held from the body or the direction in which it is pointed. The patient must try various distances and orientations of the crystal for himself until he feels an appropriate response. The exact response may be a lessening of pain or dis-comfort; a fluttering feeling around the diseased area; heat; cold; or simply a feeling of well-being. As always the best clue is what feels 'right'.

The use of crystals in *chakra healing* and balancing is common. The techniques of both contact and absent healing are equally applicable to the chakras. Once again, it is up to the healer to experiment with various crystals and to be sensitive to their effects. Many healers will discover that the crystals of certain minerals are more responsive to certain chakra energies than others. To be specific, these minerals will work *for them*. Other healers, because of the different energy relationship they have with their patients, may well discover that when they use the exact same minerals, nothing happens.

As to which crystals are best for which chakras, there is no definite answer. People who use colour for chakra healing will already know that there is no agreement on which colour to use: the same is true of crystals. Some healers have found that, again *for them*, certain crystals work best. Certain of these healers have written crystal books and listed these crystals. Maybe they will work for you, and maybe they will not – the answer lies in the sensitivity of the healer to the patient's energies and the crystal's resonance, and with his ability to match the two in a given situation. Other healers have tried using a crystal similar in colour to the colours they have been using for chakra healing, but this is simply a point of departure. Yet other healers use just one type of crystal, such as quartz, and then 'tune' each crystal to a particular chakra. There is nothing wrong with this, except that using only one mineral rather limits the range of energy responses available (recall the discussion of auras in Chapter 6). The specifics of chakras and chakra healing are covered in Chapter 10.

Acupuncture and acupressure

Crystals have a wide range of applications when combined with acupressure and acupuncture techniques. There are several diagnostic techniques available to determine areas of weakness in the various lines of energy which flow through the body, but whatever method of diagnosis is being used, treatment with crystals will often show immediate results. Crystals can be held in the hand while acupressure is being applied, or they can be directly applied to the acupressure points in place of finger contact. If you are going to use this technique, though, it is recommended that the point of the crystal be rounded off with sandpaper, as the sharp point is likely to puncture the skin. Remember to cleanse the crystal of the shock of grinding its point. In acupuncture a crystal can be used in contact with the needle, or be held in the hand as the needle is placed into the body.

Harry Oldfield, a London practitioner of crystal healing, has invented a device consisting of a white-sound frequency generator connected to a hollow glass tube filled with various crystals and a saline solution. The white sound is translated into an electric current, which passes through the tube (or 'wand'), stimulating the crystals. The wand is then placed against the body, usually at an acupressure or acupuncture point. There seems to be a response between the wand and the body's physical make-up, especially bone tissue. Results in treating a wide range of complaints have been good.

Physical injuries

Certain types of injuries to the body, particularly those involving the bone structure, tend to cause disturbances of the body's energy field that last longer than some other types of injuries, such as those to the skin or muscles. This is due to the crystalline nature of the bones themselves – remember they are organically created versions of the mineral apatite – and the fact that pain or injury tends to 'programme' itself into the bone structure as it occurs. This is also true in the case of arthritis, which can be caused by the degeneration of the crystalline material of the joint surfaces. In either case, what is important is that the bone material *itself* is programmed with disease, so treatment with crystals becomes more a matter of de-programming. In this instance, you would programme your crystal with the intention of extracting from the bone tissue the unharmonious programming. The same applies with broken bones. In all of these instances, you will probably find certain positions of the crystal will feel better than others. If crystals are applied immediately after an injury has been treated by ordinary medical means (such as setting the bone), there may be a lessening of pain when the crystal is facing some directions rather than others.

This is one time when frequent cleansing of the crystal is necessary. It is especially important that, when using a crystal to relieve the trauma programmed into broken bones, you leave in the bone the programme that deals with the re-knitting of the bone tissue. Not only that, but programme another crystal to reinforce this message.

For cuts and other types of wounds where the skin is punctured, once appropriate measures have been taken to stop the bleeding, it may be found that crystals can be helpful in reducing shock and in starting the regeneration of the injured tissues. Normally the crystal is placed in proximity to the wound and the patient is asked to breath deeply. This will help to lessen the effects of shock, since the crystal works in the subtle bodies where the symptoms of shock manifest themselves most. There is also a reduction in pain and the crystal will act as a link between both sides of the wound, so that the programming of the subtle bodies to begin healing can take place at once. Once again, the positioning of the crystal is important, and it may be necessary to move the crystal in various directions until an effect is felt. If no effect is felt by the patient, then just use the crystal in any orientation that feels comfortable to the user.

Use this same technique after surgery, but apply the healing from the deepest levels outward. Here you should intend supplementing the body's own natural healing programme, rather than trying to impose one of your own. But *do* use the crystal to 'de-programme' the trauma of the operation from the tissue, as this trauma often blocks the natural healing process. If the patient has used a crystal for meditation, by all means have them use it at this time in a meditative state to help realign the subtle bodies, which are often badly out of line due to the effects of anaesthetics. Rebalancing the energy of the chakras is particularly useful at this point.

One other crystal-healing method that should be mentioned here is one that is particularly in use in the East. Often crystals are crushed to a powder and taken internally. *Under no circumstances should you do this!* Remember, the power of the crystal is the result of its internal form: by destroying that form, you destroy the most beneficial effects. But more specifically, *some crystals can be poisonous.*

Absent healing

In absent healing, either by individuals or by groups, the use of a crystal as a focus of will and intention is particularly powerful. The crystals supplement whatever technique the healer is already using. If colour is being used, then send it through the crystal. If visualization is used, try visualizing the person inside the crystal with all of its harmonizing influences. Just holding the crystal while healing is sent is also effective. One healer has had good results by using a photograph of the patient, and placing the crystal on top of it with the appropriate intention.

The crystals used in these situations are often described as 'transmitters' of energy, but that term is totally misleading: a radio transmitter broadcasts powerful electromagnetic waves (radio waves), whereas a crystal merely serves as a point of focus for the energy bodies of the healer or healers. Absent healing may take place at any distance: subtle energies are not susceptible to the limitations of time and space, so the distance at which absent healing takes place is not important. This is another reason why the crystal has appeared to some to 'transmit' the healing energy.

The various healing techniques described in this section are by no means all-inclusive, and are merely presented to serve as a guide. Every healer will develop his or her own techniques, and there are an infinite number of combinations and variations.

Self-healing

If you are advising someone on self-healing, or seeking self-healing yourself, the question of choosing the proper crystal is sometimes more difficult. The person seeking healing may not be particularly in touch with their intuition – or they may be inclined to disbelieve it when he or she is. Nonetheless, it is still preferable for the patient to choose his or her own crystal. It is desirable to have a good selection of crystals available, allowing the patient to select the individual crystal which is in greatest harmony with their own particular energy. The question may arise that, if you are choosing a crystal in harmony with your own energy, won't that crystal necessarily harmonize with the energies of the illness? The answer is no: because intuition – an aspect of our *higher* being – is used in this selection process, it always knows our needs.

This still does not solve the problem of the person who is unaware of or indifferent to his or her intuitive powers. There are several techniques for reaching the intuitive level. As previously mentioned, almost all of us have had the experience of 'first impressions' – that feeling you get on meeting a new person or a new situation, that you often try to talk yourself out of later on, but that always proves correct in the end.

Trusting your intuition is particularly useful when selecting crystals (as was previously described in Chapter 8). As we have seen, there are several ways to apply this technique. The first is simply to shut your eyes, relax for a second or two, open your eyes and grab the first crystal that comes into your awareness. If there are several crystals that you are immediately drawn to, set them apart and use the same method again on this group. You can also choose a number of crystals that you are drawn to – for whatever reason – and then use the 'first-impression' method.

It is often enough simply to reach into a box of crystals with your eyes closed and take out whatever crystal the hand is led to. There is nothing wrong with using this method with your eyes open, but it is often tempting to choose the 'prettier' one that is next to the crystal that you *really* feel drawn to! Again, there is that element of 'first impression', that is, making your choice before you actually have a chance to *think* about what you are doing.

If you are choosing your crystals from someone who already works with them, there is certainly nothing wrong with allowing them to aid you in your choice. Ask them to pick out a dozen or so crystals which their intuition suggests might be helpful, and then make your final choice from those – keeping in mind once again that the final choice is *always* yours; even though the 'professional' may have chosen a certain group of crystals, it could still be that *none* of his or her choices will feel 'right'.

The actual techniques of self-healing with a crystal are easy enough – placing the crystal in the aura either by wearing it, holding it in the hand and passing it through the aura, or perhaps even placing it under your pillow or bed when you are sleeping. Again it is a matter of whatever feels right to the patient. It cannot be emphasized enough that the techniques of crystal healing are not meant to replace other types of treatment such as homeopathy, acupuncture and orthodox medical practice, but rather to supplement them.

Mental Illness

The use of crystals to heal mental disorders has been little practiced, but in that we recognize the unity of mind, body and spirit, as a consequence we also recognize that there is no such thing as purely 'mental' illness. Research by physicians and psychiatrists such as Dr Arthur Janov (discoverer of Primal Therapy) clearly demonstrates that so-called mental illnesses, and, in particular, those that are not a direct result of malfunctions of the brain, all have physical components elsewhere in the body. It follows that however any given mental illness originates, any and all of them will have energetic components represented in the patient's aura. As such, the illnesses are susceptable to crystal treatment. Note, however, that the same cautions apply to the treatment of 'mental' illness as 'physical' illness: use crystals to supplement and complement other therapies, *not* to replace them.

The physical brain and psychiatric conditions that are directly related to its malfunction – such as Seasonal Affective Disorder (SAD) – can be very receptive to crystal healing because there is harmony between the crystals of organic nature (the brain) and the crystals of inorganic nature used in healing. To begin healing damaged brain tissue, or at least re-programming undiseased brain tissue to take over the functions of the damaged areas, the crystal should be programmed with the intention of re-programming the brain cells, and then applied directly to the head in whatever location feels best to the patient. This method can be particularly useful in treating diseases such as alcoholism, which have a long-term degenerative effect on brain tissue. For general healing of mental disorders, if we recognize that the total energy field and its overall balance will reflect whatever levels of energy are involved in the disorder, then programming a crystal with a general balancing programme can be beneficial. The actual placement/carrying/wearing of the crystal or crystals will be the same as if treating a 'physical' illness.

The techniques discussed in the treatment of the brain and in mental illness can also be used in self-healing, but the actual programming of the crystals used by the patient might be best done by a healer, or by a disinterested party. Obviously if the patient has some degree of mental disturbance, it may be difficult for him or her to programme clearly the crystal for the self-healing process. (It is also necessary that patients use common sense, recognizing that if they continue to fill their body with caffeine, sugar and other unhealthy substances, then all the healing techniques in the world are ultimately doomed to fail!)

Advice for New Crystal Healers

To the therapist starting out in practice, there are a few things that need to be considered.

1   ***Training****.Training is all well and good, but remember: what you are offering in the final analysis is your skill as a healer, a skill that goes far beyond any technical information or healing techniques you may learn.*

2   ***Limitations****. Recognize that you have limitations in what you can realistically and ethically do in your practice:*

- *Never, ever, suggest that a patient ceases to use prescription medication, stop a prescribed regimen by a doctor or other health professional, or cancel or ignore any other prescribed course of treatment. Aside from the purely ethical aspects of this, there are some very severe legal aspects as well.*

- *Never, ever, diagnose. That is to say, never offer a diagnosis for a symptom or group of symptoms that might prevent the patient from seeking orthodox medical advice. You may, for example, diagnose recurrent headaches as imbalances in the chakra energies of the crown; the patient may, in fact, have a brain tumour. By all means treat the energy imbalances, which will undoubtedly exist if there is a brain tumour, but do nothing more than this.*

- *Where a medical diagnosis already exists, never, ever, tell your patient the diagnosis is wrong and the illness is due to something else.*

3   **Litigation**. *Be aware that in countries such as the USA where litigation is a way of life, certain actions on your part may be misinterpreted. Always fully explain your treatment and what you are about to undertake, and never, ever, touch a patient without asking their permission. This includes laying crystals on the body. Always be aware of how any action you undertake might be misinterpreted. It is recommended that you video, or at least audio-tape, each session as a safeguard both for yourself and the patient. This is not necessarily a negative thing: it is also invaluable as the patient reports results back to you, to see exactly what you did in the healing process that achieved those results. Always inform the patient that the sessions are being recorded.*

4   ***Opposite-sex patients***. *Treating patients of the opposite sex is a potential minefield. Aside from possible misinterpretation of your actions, in some countries there are severe legal limitations on the type of relationship you can maintain with your patient outside of the therapeutic environment.*

5   ***Legal position***. *Be aware that in some countries, complementary practice is seriously limited legally.*

Other considerations for healers

There are a few important points to remember yourself, and to emphasize to your patients:

- *Healing does not* begin *in the physical body but in the subtle bodies, of which the physical body is only a reflection; since crystals are capable of reflecting energies from the lowest to the highest, it becomes possible to treat a number of subtle bodies simultaneously.*

- *It is important that crystals are not 'taken' like pills. The nature of* healing, *as opposed to medicine, is the difference between* sensing *what a*

133

patient needs (through the intuition) and thinking about what the patient needs (the process of rational thought). The true healer, whether he or she uses crystals or not, principally operates through the intuitive link with the patient. Since the energies of the subtle bodies, like the interaction with the crystal itself, can only be sensed through intuition, it is only through such sensitivity that true healing using crystals take place.

- In healing with crystals, it does not seem to matter whether the crystal is in its natural state or whether it has been shaped. Obviously sawing a crystal in two will change its resonance, but as long as the crystals are properly cleansed to remove any energy disturbance resulting from the cutting, they seem to work just as effectively. This also includes crystals which have been cut as gems.

Other Types of Crystal Healing

Healing plants and animals

Healing animals with crystals is no different from healing humans, apart from actually placing the crystals. For an animal too ill to move, this is less of a problem, but few animals will sit or lie still long enough to place crystals directly on them. Most healers who work with animals hold the crystal in their hand while performing contact healing. Crystals can be placed in an animal's bed or stall as well. For larger animals with backbones, the same methods of sensing auric energy and the chakra points described in Chapter 10 generally apply.

The same cautions apply to the use of crystals with animals as with humans: never supersede the advice, treatment or medication of a veterinary doctor, or make any diagnosis that would cause the owner or keeper of the animal to not seek proper veterinary care.

Crystals can be used in conjunction with the Plant Kingdom. For example, if you have problems in the garden, programme a perfect image of the garden into a crystal, and place or bury the crystal in an appropriate spot in the garden. Again, your own sensitivity will tell you where the crystal needs to be, and the direction in which it should face. For ill plants either in the garden or in the house, programme a crystal to support the plant's natural healing energy and leave it next to the plant. Once again, it will be necessary for the gardener to attune to various attributes of plant growth and healing to see which crystals are in harmony. Or, why not programme a crystal to supplement the vital energies of plant growth, and plant one with your seeds in the Spring?

Planetary healing

There is one last type of healing that needs to be mentioned. Many people who are being drawn to work with crystals today are truly hearing the call of the planet and the cosmos to once again begin to understand this level of energy, and to interact with it properly. This book is a direct outgrowth of that call, and those who are drawn to read it will be responding to the same call. Although a discussion of past lives is beyond the scope of this book, many of those who are drawn to work with crystals believe themselves to have used them before, some correctly, and some incorrectly. In past life memories crystals were used in many cultures and civilizations, particularly the one remembered by many as Atlantis. These memories essentially recall a time of misuse, for which many, if not all, of the misusers are atoning today through their opportunities for proper use. How is it going to go *this* time? Watch this space.

One of the major works to be undertaken by New Age centres is that of consciously working to rebalance and reharmonize planetary energies. It is necessary here to mention also the Earth changes that are being forecast by many seers. Many involve land-mass changes, some of which could be as dramatic as the Earth's readjustment during Atlantean times. One thing that must be emphasized is that these changes are the last resort of the planet, and will occur only if man is unable to make the proper planetary adjustments himself. We can be assured that these changes will take place only in the last second of the 11th hour, and will only take place in proportion to what man himself has not done for the planet. In either case, the needs of the planet will be fulfilled, but it will certainly be a great deal more comfortable for us if we can relieve the planet of the necessity to create its own adjustments!

Balance and harmony are the things most lacking in the world today; and yet we live on a world that is *made* of crystals, with their natural tendency for harmony. Someone once calculated (and the writer has checked) that the entire human race could fit into a cube a half-mile (0.8 kilometre) long on each edge. If there are any doubts about the ability of mankind to influence the Earth in a positive way, we need only look around us to see how much disharmony this minute fragment of the whole of the Earth Being has caused.

However, the potential for harmony is there also, and perhaps with this perspective of how much of the physical Earth we occupy, we can begin to see how only a small portion of mankind working for the good of the planet can create changes far out of proportion to their numbers – especially when combined with the universal connection of crystals. In undertaking planetary healing with crystals there are two things to remember: there is nothing in the chemical components of our physical body that does not come from the Earth; it is, therefore, utterly and totally part of the planet. The crystal, as something which is part of and (for the most part *is*) the Earth's body, becomes a direct physical link between the two.

An ancient Greek once said: 'Give me a long enough lever and a place to stand, and I will move the Earth.' What he didn't say is that the fulcrum of that lever need have been no larger than a pea! A clear example of how this sort of small application of power can have results far beyond the apparent size of the object itself, was given to the writer during a visit to Egypt, when he was asked to place a small, specially-shaped crystal at a particular point of power in one of the old Egyptian temples. Having managed to do so, on leaving the temple he was worried about the crystal being found and removed, and asked 'How long does it have to be in place?'

The reply came back, 'How long does it take a match to start a forest fire?'

TEN

EXERCISES

The exercises in this chapter are directed both at the person under-taking self-healing, and at the therapist giving treatment. For the healer, the visualizations may be read aloud to the patient who, in a relaxed or meditative state, performs the suggested actions. These visualizations have worked well for the author, and other therapists are invited to use them freely.

As this book has emphasized, true healing takes place in the deep-est inner levels of our being – the levels most of us tend to be out of touch with for most of the time in our busy world. There is a potent need within each of us to be one with the natural world around us, but this is the very need most ignored in the hurly-burly of everyday life. It can but enrich each of our lives to take a few min-utes each day to reconnect with the flow of nature. Meditation – a few minutes of quiet reflection – is a good way to do this. It puts us back in touch not only with the roots of our being, but also with the levels of ourselves in which health and well-being lie. Meditation is, moreover, a good first point of contact with the mineral level of con-sciousness. It is also a starting point for the powerful visualization techniques of this chapter. These techniques are well-proven meth-ods of addressing the deep inner levels that are the source of health and healing.

Meditation

Many readers will already practice some form of meditation, so just add visualization and meditation with crystals into what you are already doing. For those who have not meditated or done visualiza-tions, the following steps are suggested:

1   *Create a sacred space*. The whole world is a
    sacred place, but our lives have become so
    intense, practical and economic in their
    orientation that the claims of the moment are
    often so great we hardly know where we are.
    Creating a personal, sacred space is necessary,
    whether you meditate in it or where you can
    simply go to experience and bring forth what
    you are and what you might be. It can be a
    room, or it need be nothing more than a
    certain hour or so in the day, or some music
    that you really love. The purpose of your
    sacred space is get the feeling of connection
    to life, so it can become a place of creative
    incubation, whether for healing or any other
    life-sustaining activity.

2   *Get comfortable*. You can sit on a chair or on
    the floor. Lying down is not recommended as it
    is too easy to go to sleep! Arrange your legs in
    the most comfortable position if you are sitting
    on the floor – there is no need to bend yourself
    double to sit in the lotus position. If you choose
    to sit on a chair, sit with your legs uncrossed
    with your feet flat on the floor. In either
    position, keep your back as straight as possible
    and fold your hands comfortably in your lap.

3   *Breathe*. Take a deep breath and let it out
    slowly. Do the same again. Relax, let your
    shoulders drop, and focus on the rise and fall
    of your chest. Your eyes will close of their

own accord, and your breathing will naturally start to slow. Up to this point, you are practising a relaxation technique that is good for dealing with stress, and you can use it for that at any time.

4   ***Visualization or meditation****. When you are relaxed, you can start the suggested visualization. If you are meditating for information, focus on your crystal and direct the question in its direction, whether it is in your hand or elsewhere. What you are really focusing on is the crystal's reflection of yourself, and your question is, in reality, the programme. You are in complete control of your experience, and can stop at any time. This is not hypnosis or anything similar, it is just relaxation.*

Suggested techniques and applications

Because many readers will be new to crystals, meditating with them is a good starting point. The actual meditation technique can be nothing more than holding a crystal in your hand, or crystals of different minerals in each hand. You can place a crystal on the floor in front of you or on a small table, where you can focus on it as you meditate. Another technique is to place a number of crystals in a circle on the floor, and sit in the centre of the circle. The actual choice of crystals is quite personal: they can all be of one mineral, such as quartz or amethyst, or be a mixture of different minerals. This technique of forming a circle of crystals can also be used to 'programme' another crystal by placing it in the centre of the circle.

It is often a good idea to meditate with a newly acquired crystal, especially if you are not clear why it has come to you. In this meditation, 'ask' the crystal what uses it is in harmony with and what it would like to be used for. The response may be an intuitive feeling, a vision of a particular use, or perhaps even a sensation of a 'verbal' reply. Just leave your mind open to whatever happens. How can an inanimate object tell us anything? It can't – it is just reflecting back to you the dimension of yourself wherein the answer lies.

Meditation is also a good way to discover the specific techniques and uses of crystals that are right for you. If you are a person who visualizes easily, while meditating ask to be shown, in as much detail as necessary, exactly how to use your crystals. If you are not particularly visual, you may get a sense, or even 'hear' directions. A specialized form of meditation is suggested later in the chapter, to set in motion the inner processes for healing.

Sensing and Working With the Aura

Rather than interacting with auras in a general sense, when you begin crystal healing it is possible to focus on specific areas which are in need of attention. Although only a limited number of people are able visually to see auras, virtually everyone can sense them. As we saw in Chapter 2, such sensing happens all the time. How sensitive we all are can be demonstrated with a simple experiment.

Find a quiet place to do this, where other energies of daily life do not intrude. Find a friend who is sympathetic to the process and stand facing each other, a foot or so apart. Both of you raise your hands to shoulder height, palms outward, with your hands palm to palm, just a few inches apart. In a short while, you will feel a pulsing flowing between your palms and theirs. This is the natural pulse of your mutual energy fields. Now, move your hands back so that they are a foot or so apart. You will still feel the pulsation. Now, both of you take a step backward, keeping your hands opposite each other. The pulsation will still be there. One of you then move your hands from side to side, slowly. The other person will be able to feel at which point the energy pulse can no longer be felt. Swap roles. Now each of you take another step backwards, and repeat the process. And so on again. It works best for most people if eye contact is maintained throughout. At some point when the pulsing is strong, try closing your eyes in turn to see how it may or may not affect the pulse. It isn't unusual to be able to feel the pulsation the width of a room or more apart. This simple experiment demonstrates two things: how sensitive we are to auras when we really focus, and how far our own and the auras of others extend. It also demonstrates why we can respond to a total stranger across a crowded room – the old songs have got it right!

Lilian Verner-Bonds suggests a simple exercise to start consciously seeing auras. Begin by looking just to the side of the head of the person you are working with, and allow your eyes to go out of focus. Most people will first see a light gray or silver band an inch or two wide, surrounding the head, which relates to the electrical processes of the body. You can begin to get information about the person's state of health even from this layer. A bright, light gray indicates generally good health, but black or slate grey indicates a depleted energy state. With practice, colours will eventually appear, although many people will not see them visually but, rather, will 'sense' them.[1]

[1] Lilian Verner-Bonds, *The Complete Book of Color Healing* (London: Godsfield, 2000).

In a more therapeutic surrounding, you can sense fluctuations or blockages in the energy field of the person undergoing treatment. Seat them in a chair – wood or plastic is better than metal, which may interact with the aura – and run your hand slowly up and down their spine, about four inches (10cms) from their body. The person's energies are just as strong at the back as well as the front of the body, and it is easier and more comfortable for the patient if you work from the back. If you have done the previous experiment, you will be aware of the energy pulse from the seated person, and if you work slowly and take time to focus, you will be able to feel where the pulse is stronger or weaker, or where it changes tempo. Alternatively, you may only feel a sensation of heat, which will vary according to where the person's energy is weak or is blocked. Strong energy blocks will feel quite hot, and will feel noticeably different from the surrounding temperatures. The reason for working along the spine is that the body's energies focus at certain points along the spine, called *chakras*.

The Chakras

There are seven major points at which the body's energies interface with the energies of its surroundings. These are called *chakras*, the 'seven centres' that are points of focus of various levels of energy along the spine, neck and head. Because energy comes in many shapes and forms like heat, light, inertia, momentum and so on, it follows that as physical, mental, emotional and spiritual beings, we too embody many different levels of energy, and that within the levels we embody exists a spectrum of energies. The term 'levels of energy' can be misleading: for many it conjures up a vision of layers in a cake! However, a better model would be billions of spheres of energy, ranging from smaller than a grain of sand to the size of

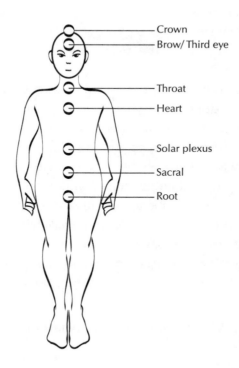

Crown
Brow/ Third eye
Throat
Heart
Solar plexus
Sacral
Root

Figure 8: The seven chakra points

golf balls, all uniformly intermixed. All a chakra does is selectively filter out all but the right size for the energy purpose that particular chakra serves. The locations of the chakras are shown in Figure 8.

It is worth repeating: our chakras and energy fields are not purely things by themselves. Mind, body and spirit exist both as part of, and as a field of energy in their own right. The greater energy is the energy of the Earth and the Cosmos, but within that field of energy they exist as part of an individual being unique unto themselves.

Various names are given to these different yet interconnected levels and dimensions of energy, depending on which philosophy, religion or science is doing the describing.

The aura is often seen as a field of energy composed of a number of colours extending beyond the physical body; the exact colours depend on the person's mood, state of mind and, more importantly, state of health. Chakras are often linked to the colour spectrum: at one end are the purely physical energies of matter and reproduction – usually described as 'dense' and related to the colour red. At the other end are the 'higher' energies of purple, which are lighter, more subtle and easily overlooked in everyday life. Between these points are five other levels, each of which relate to a different facet of life. The human attributes embodied by the chakras can be strengthened or emphasized through raising the energy of the associated chakra.

Table 2: Chakras and their associations

The first three chakras are linked to the body's physical survival:

Chakra	Location	Colour	Association
Root Chakra	Pelvic bone	Red	Sexuality, Survival, Reproduction, Travel
Sacral Chakra	Lower abdomen	Orange	'Gut level' Emotion, Creativity, Work, Career Opportunities, Divorce
Solar Plexus Chakra	Solar Plexus	Yellow	Self-esteem, Relationships, Social Identity, Intellectual Accomplishments, Examinations

The next three chakra locations are the heart, throat and brow, and the seventh chakra, the crown, is located at the top of the head:

Heart Chakra	Heart	Green	The Emotions, Love, Self-acceptance, Acceptance of Others, General Health
Throat Chakra	Throat	Blue	Communication, Self-expression, Voicing Opinions
Brow Chakra	Midway between the eyes	Indigo	Intuition, Insight, Physic Abilities
Crown Chakra	Top of the head	Purple	Spiritual Connection, Spiritual Opening and Understanding, Leadership Qualities, Artistic Possibilities

Healing and Strengthening the Aura and Chakras

Imbalances in the energy field, and in particular those that are severe enough to result in disease, will always be associated with imbalances in the chakras associated with that particular level or levels of energy. They can therefore be sensed by the above technique. There will be disturbances in the remainder of the energy field as well, but these are often less easy to sense, which is why working through the chakras is recommended for those beginning their healing work. As your sensitivities develop, you will be able to go directly to the exact point.

There are several techniques for working with chakra energy, and, with experience, most healers will develop their own; thus if you are receiving crystal healing, don't be surprised if your healer uses different techniques. If you are giving crystal healing, there is a series of choices that need to be made. You can make them in turn, and at the particular moment, dictated by what 'feels right', or you can work through the choices in a standard order that you know works for you. The first step is to choose an appropriate crystal or crystals. This in turn depends on whether you are going to balance or strengthen the chakras.

Balancing the chakras

The first thing you will discover is that rarely is only one chakra out of balance. Because the chakras are reflections of the whole of the energy body, if one part is unbalanced, others are likely to be too. Therefore the next criterion in choosing your crystals is: do I use one crystal for all of the chakras or a different one for each? Either option is perfectly acceptable. Your choice will be dictated solely by your instinct at the time about which of the two options 'feels right'.

If you are drawn to use only one crystal, then you are ready. If you are drawn to use several – perhaps one for each chakra – then there are other options. You can use the same type of crystal for each chakra – all quartz or all topaz, for example – selecting individual crystals that 'feel right' for each chakra in turn. Alternatively, you can use a different type of crystal for each chakra. This generates another set of choices: you can choose each individual crystal solely on the 'feels right' basis without regard to its colour, or, you can choose from a selection of crystals that are the colour associated with the particular chakras you are treating. (Balancing chakras is a good place to begin consciously working with the colour in crystals.) Again, either option is valid, depending on what 'feels right'.

Having chosen your crystal or crystals, the next set of choices is how to actually use them: place them on or around the patient, hold them yourself, or have the patient hold them.

If you place the crystals on or around the patient, programme them to balance and harmonize the patient's energy, with the intention of activating the patient's own inner resources. Placing crystals in this manner is usually easiest if the patient is lying down. Remember that the act of placing crystals on the body requires touching the patient, and permission should be obtained beforehand, after a full explanation of what you are proposing to do. In particular, be sure to tell them *where* you are going to place the crystals. This is especially important if it is the first encounter with a new patient.

As noted in a previous chapter, the direction each crystal will point depends on precisely where it is placed. You will need to turn each crystal through a complete circle as you place it, to see in which direction it 'feels right'. If you are using a coloured crystal, place it on the afflicted chakra or area. In addition, visualize a flow of the appropriate colour flowing into the area you are treating.

If you hold the crystals yourself, then the programme should reflect your own involvement; or, more correctly, your intention about the degree to which your own energies are involved in the balancing and healing process. If you are using one crystal for more than one chakra you may or may not feel the need to reprogramme the crystal for each chakra. Both methods are appropriate, according to how you sense the need. The crystal can then be held in the chakra energy, either in contact with the body or at a distance from it. The four-inch (10cm) distance seems to be fairly common. The crystal can be held still or rotated, depending on the 'feels right' sense in the moment. The same series of actions apply if different crystals are used, either different crystals of the same mineral, or of different minerals altogether. If using a coloured crystal, visualize a flow of colour through it, as before.

An alternative to the healer holding the crystal is to have the patient hold the crystal or crystals themselves. Have them place the crystal at the various chakra points, and rotate them or not as intuitively sensed. You can programme the crystals or, if the patient is happy to do so, they can do it themselves. This technique is also invaluable for self-healing, and does not require the presence of a 'healer'.

Pendulum balancing

A simple technique for chakra balancing is to use a crystal pendulum over each chakra spot on the body. You can use a colourless crystal, but to balance and give an extra boost to each chakra you can use a same-coloured crystal pendulum as the chakra. You can sit the person in a chair or have them lie down, as before. Hold your chosen crystal suspended from a chain or piece of string, and allow the pendulum to swing in front of, if the patient is sitting, or over, if lying down, each chakra in turn, starting at the base and working up. The pendulum may swing wildly at first, turning in either direction; if so, wait until it settles down and stops, showing that the chakra is balanced. You can also use a pendulum on yourself.

Strengthening the chakras

Sometimes, rather than sensing a disturbance or imbalance in a chakra or chakras, you will just sense that one or more of them feels weak. To strengthen a chakra with crystals, use exactly the same technique as that for balancing them described above. The difference will be in the programme, which will be for boosting chakra energy, rather than balancing it. The other difference will be that when you choose the crystal or crystals, it is likely that you will choose different ones than for balancing. But you need do nothing more than focus your intention for strengthening rather than balancing the chakras when you choose your crystals, and your 'feels right' feelings will do the rest. This technique is also good for boosting the energies associated with the various facets of life attributed to the various chakras, shown in Table 2, above.

As noted in Chapter 9, numerous variations on the above techniques are possible. Although this chapter has suggested beginning your healing work with the chakras, the techniques described above can be applied anywhere on the body. Chakras were suggested as a starting point because the energies are more strongly focused there, and are therefore easier to sense.

Visualization

While the above techniques are good for healing and balancing the energy field from 'outside', visualization is a powerful tool for setting in motion the inner changes that are ultimately necessary for perfect healing. A combination of both is recommended. Visualization is nothing more than creative imagining, while in a relaxed state. The human mind operates in symbols – as it is doing

151

right now as you read the symbolic markings the mind interprets as letters and words. Written words, which are, after all, nothing more than patterns of ink on paper can, if arranged properly, make us laugh or cry, arouse or depress us. It is the clearest demonstration possible of the power of symbols. Thus in visualization, the power of symbols is combined with the naturally higher state of receptivity to suggestion brought about by a relaxed state. Clearly, the choice of symbols is important. The symbols used in these visualizations have been tried and tested in many courses and therapeutic sessions, and are likely to achieve useful results. They will not do so for everyone, because every human mind is unique. If they do not work for you, alter them or create new visualizations based on them that are meaningful to you.

The first visualization focuses on the Heart Centre, which corresponds with the Heart Chakra. There, within each of us, is that perfect place that is always One with the Heart of God. Both hearts not only beat to the same inner pulse, both hearts *are* the same pulse. The more we retain our inner harmony and natural rhythm, the more we reharmonize with the source of our being – God, in whatever form we perceive him to be. Opening the heart is to seek truth at its deepest level: the truth of who you are. True health and healing cannot occur otherwise. Within the Heart Centre is the place where the fundamental patterns of creation are at their clearest, and it is the place most clearly reflected in those other fundamental patterns of creation: crystals. Here is where we discover the other levels of consciousness which already exist within ourselves, the levels particularly reflected back to us in crystals.

As your heart reopens, as you begin to find and expose deeper and deeper levels of Truth, what will change most dramatically is your perspective. You will realize that you are your own source of healing, of personal power, of the creation of your own life around you. Fortunately, the process of opening the heart is a process of gradual unfoldment – we are so conditioned to not see those things within us, that were we to see the Truth all at once, we wouldn't believe it!

The format of the visualizations is as follows: first, a statement of the purpose of the exercise – what the exercise is intended to accomplish; second, the crystal for the exercise – a specific crystal is not suggested, because it will be different for each person, what is recommended is the *purpose* you should have in mind when choosing an appropriate crystal; and third, the programme – your focus of intention for performing the exercise. There will also be introductory material explaining the function of the exercise.

During these exercises, it is likely that you will experience physical sensations in the area of the heart, feelings of radiating warmth, of softness, of melting, and indeed, you may also experience physical discomfort. Should you do so, there is no need for alarm. The psychological and energetic armouring that covers our hearts is held in place by severe muscular tension in the chest area. As we begin to let go of the energetic armour, those muscles will begin to relax. It is like setting down a heavy load that you have been carrying for longer than you wished – when you finally put it down, you notice how tight and cramped the muscles are. This is not to suggest that you should not seek competent medical advice should you feel any sense of discomfort or alarm about any of the physical sensations that occur in any of the exercises in the book. You should.

A healing note on forgiveness: That which we fail to forgive binds us. But forgiveness, real forgiveness, comes from a deep realization that those with whom we have issues have been our teachers – just as we asked them to be at some deep level. The closer we can come to that realization, the more we can recognize that, in the end, there is nothing to forgive. This recognition seldom comes quickly, but the following exercises can set that energy in motion.

The first exercise is about cleansing the Heart Centre, and is designed to set in motion, subconsciously, powerful energetic forces in your own Being that will facilitate the remaining exercises in this book.

Exercise 1: Heart-cleansing visualization

Purpose

This is an exercise for symbolically cleansing the Heart Centre, to set in motion inner processes that will start to eliminate the inner barriers that keep us from the full experience of life, and which are the ultimate source of illness. In it you are using the crystal as a symbol of the perfect Inner Being that dwells in the depth of your heart, and the technique is to clear away anything that is clouding the perfect Inner Being – all thoughts, feelings and beliefs that are not in perfect harmony with who you are. This will all be visualized in symbols; you may see inharmonious beliefs as tiny bits of rubbish, as black gunk, or as some sort of scattered debris. Just let your own mind create whatever symbol works the best for you.

Crystal

The crystal for this exercise will be placed directly over the Heart Centre, and you will be projecting yourself into the crystal. In choosing a crystal for this exercise find one with which you feel a deep heart connection.

Programme

This crystal is programmed to reflect back to you the deepest levels of your own perfection, and, by contrast, for you to be able to see all of those things in your heart – in whatever symbols are appropriate to you – that keep it from being clear and clean and a perfect source of love to all of your being.

Exercise

With the crystal in place over your heart, take in a few deep breaths and let them out slowly. As you do, become aware of your own heartbeat. Focus initially on the heartbeat, rather than the crystal. As you become more and more focused on your heartbeat, feel that heartbeat as the centre of your being, as if everything that you are is focused in that beat. And as you become more and more focused on the heart, then extend your awareness to include the crystal resting on it.

As you become more and more focused on the crystal, visualize the crystal becoming larger and larger, and your body becoming smaller and smaller. Eventually the crystal will become larger than your body, and you can then allow yourself to slip inside the crystal. It is as if we are stepping inside your own heart, the symbol of which is the crystal.

When you are inside the crystal, take a moment to sense the feeling of utter balance and perfection inside, and just look around. Experience being in your crystal as if being inside a room – the facets of the crystal are the walls of the room.

When you feel comfortable inside the room, notice that in one of the walls (one of the faces of the crystal) there is a window. You can see this as any sort of window you like – a porthole, a large window, a small window – but in any instance one that can be opened. Walk to the window and open it. And as you look out of the window, you will see that what is outside is … the Cosmos. A whole universe of stars outside the window.

The universe is the source of everything in our Being – the unbalanced thoughts and beliefs, as well as the balanced ones. Our unbalanced thoughts and feelings are ones which have taught us: they are the things which have propelled us into learning. But as we begin to reach out to reharmonize ourselves with the universe, we no longer need these things, so it is OK to return them to the universe.

So, have a look around inside your heart crystal, looking for anything that looks out of balance, anything that is not in harmony. As mentioned, you may see it as rubbish or litter, or of some sort of muck. You will find at hand whatever tools you need to clean with – so set to it! As you clean up whatever rubbish you find inside, just shovel it out of the window; return it to the Cosmos.

As you go on cleaning, you will see the whole place becoming tidier; it begins to take on a bright and shiny, brand-new sort of look. You may even want to take a cloth and polish it!

When you have finished cleaning, close your window and return your cleaning tools to their proper place.

When you have completed all of this, begin taking deeper and deeper breaths focusing on your heartbeat. As you do so, visualize the crystal becoming smaller and smaller and your body becoming larger and larger, until you have both returned to your proper size.

One of the favourite exercises in my courses is to have each person choose a crystal that either makes the participant uncomfortable or, even better, one that they absolutely dislike. Then, by sitting and meditating while feeling the uncomfortable feelings, to get in touch with whatever aspect of themselves that it is reflecting. Use this

meditation/visualization to discover those particular aspects of yourself, and have a 'housecleaning', as above.

Exercise 2: The sacred spring visualization

A number of people (including the writer) have, in deep meditation and going further into the centre of their own being than they have ever been before, become aware of a glowing light. Within that light is a pattern, made from energy, which is light blue in colour. There is a central structure to it, which appears to be rods of light, and surrounding those rods of light are hundreds of dots of light, arranged in a very precise pattern. There is a recognition that the 'rods' are somehow the core of the structure, and that each of the blue dots is an experience. We have all experienced ourselves to be literally looking at the centre of our own Being. It is a place we can all find within ourselves.

In this exercise you will use a symbol rooted in the most ancient mythologies – a cave – to go deeply into the core of your own Being. The cave is an important symbol for the Heart Centre, for just as you go deeper and deeper into the body of the earth in a real cave, you go deeper and deeper into the body of our own Being in a symbolic cave. In the following exercise the 'cave' is man-made, but the effect is the same. The depth of inner connection you can make in this exercise is profound, and it is one that you may wish to repeat a number of times as you progress along your inward journey. What you will discover as you do so is that the inner experience, although similar or identical in form each time, will have more subtle nuances, connecting with deeper subtleties of your own Being.

Purpose
To be in touch with the deepest level of your own heart, the energy pattern that is at the core of your Being.

Crystal

Choose a crystal for this exercise to which you feel a response deep in your Heart Centre. I suggest you look for a physical sensation in the heart for this one. In this exercise, the crystal is placed over the heart.

Programme

To be drawn into the very deepest level of your own Being, and to see reflected back to you, the energy pattern that is your Beingness.

Exercise

In ancient times, the water source for a city was often within the city wall, and was reached through a very deep well. These wells were often more than just vertical shafts, they were proper tunnels, with stairs leading down into them. Our sacred spring will be in such a location.

Go in your mind then to some ancient place – a place where you feel a sacred connection. This can be a real place or an imagined one. Whatever place you go to, find a doorway, a doorway that opens into a sloping tunnel, which leads to a sacred spring. Create the kind of doorway you might expect to find in such a place: an elaborate doorway, the entrance to a temple, or whatever image you would see for such a sacred place.

As you walk up to the door, you may sense that you would like to do some sort of ritual, or some sort of personal cleansing, as you are about to enter a holy place. When you have done this, enter the doorway and begin walking downward. There is a passageway, a sloping tunnel that leads deep into the earth. It is a wide passageway, with stairs and a slope that is comfortable to walk down. It is warm and dry in this passageway, and it is spacious enough that there is no sense of confinement.

As the light of day fades behind you, the lighting in the passageway will be provided by candles, giving it a warm and soft glow. You will hear the echo of your footsteps, as you go deeper and deeper into the earth.

Give yourself plenty of time, and really try to sense the depth – deeper, and deeper, and deeper, and deeper. Eventually, when you feel you have reached the very bottom, you will begin to hear a gentle sound of water trickling. You know that you are approaching the sacred spring, and the pool that lies at its feet. As you reach the deepest part of the tunnel, you will find that it opens into a large room, with a beautiful pool of candlelit water, surrounded by a sandy beach and a number of seats. You are there by yourself, but you know that this is the same life source for many others.

Seat yourself by the pool, and just feel the energy that comes upward with the spring – the waters of life. As you look at the pool, you will eventually notice that there is a faint glow in the water which begins to get brighter as you watch it. You know that there is no fear about what you are going to see, but you certainly may have other feelings that are appropriate to express.

The glow becomes even brighter and you suddenly sense that something is rising up out of the water, from the very depths. As you watch, a glowing figure rises from the water. It is not in human form, being made up mostly of points of light, but you will be aware that radiating from this figure of light is an intense feeling of joy and love. You will realize, that in the depths of your Being, this is who you really are.

There may be some communication from this Being of light, or there may not, but in either case there will be a moment when you sense you have been in the presence of this Being for a sufficient amount of time. When you do, the Being will sink into the depths once again, leaving you alone in the candlelit chamber.

When you sense completion, allow yourself time to digest your experience, and when you are ready, return to the surface. Allow yourself plenty of time to return, and if you have experienced any deep emotional feelings during this exercise, lie down on the bed or the floor, or wherever you are meditating, on your left side, until a sense of inner peace returns.

Write down what you have seen and experienced as soon as possible after completing this exercise. Note every detail you can remember, whether those details seem important or not.

Exercise 3: Roots of illness

Purpose
To identify specific ideas and beliefs that are associated with any specific illness or injury that you have, and to set in motion the energetic phase of healing.

Crystal
A crystal on the brow and on the place where an ailment or injury has affected the body, chosen for a feeling of deep self-reflection, to mirror back to you any specific imbalance in your body energies and to connect that imbalance to a specific idea or belief.

Programme
To reflect back to you the idea, belief or early experience that is the root of a specific ailment.

Exercise

Lie on your back for this exercise. Place the crystal on the area of the body where a symptom occurs; if you have had an injury to a specific body part, then place the crystal on that area. If you have an illness that involves a particular area of the body, place the crystal on that location.

Allow your full awareness to flow into the crystal and, as you do so, you will find certain body feelings and sensations in that particular place. Allow those feelings to flow into the crystal, as if infusing it with those sensations.

Next, let the crystal expand to become much larger than your body, until it is as if you are lying in a room inside the crystal. The wall opposite you is one large mirror, fully visible from where you lie. In that mirror, an image or images will form, images constructed from the feelings you have infused into the crystal. You may see infancy or childhood events, even past-life events, or you may just see formless shapes and colours; all of these images will be somehow connected to you. Visualize these attachments symbolically – perhaps as cables or cords, or steel bars, or even as lines of energy. Notice where the attachments connect to your body.

There are several questions you need answers to at this point. When did I first experience these feelings or sensations? What event was associated with them? What belief do I have about myself as a result of this experience? Why have I given myself this illness? What actions can I take to relieve the underlying feelings that are creating this illness? And, what change in my beliefs about myself or the state of the world need to happen to release this illness? As you ask these questions, answers will form somewhere within the confines of the crystal room. You may see words form in the mirror, you may

161

see responses in the material of the connecting lines, you may hear words audibly, or you may just get impressions of answers.

When you feel complete with the answers you have received, notice a toolbox alongside you. Reach into it and pull out an appropriate tool for cutting the ties. Move your hands and physically act out the movements. When you have finished cutting them, go down your body and pull out the roots of the connections which you have just cut loose. The energetic roots may go entirely through your body, so do whatever is necessary to pull them completely out.

Then, see the connections that have been cut and the roots that have been pulled loose lying on the floor. Reach into the toolbox again and select some appropriate means of disposing of them. You may find a box of matches if the ties are made of something flammable, or if they are steel bars, you may find a laser to disintegrate them. Whatever method you choose, the bits that have been cut loose and pulled out should be totally destroyed.

After the process of destroying the connections has been completed, then replace the tools, and find a pot of healing balm – again visualizing it in a form meaningful to you. Smooth it over and into all of the places where the roots of your connections have been pulled from your body; then return the pot to its place. When all of the ties have been cut, you will see the reflection in the mirror fade away and disappear, leaving the crystal clean and clear.

When you have completed the exercise, see the crystal beginning to shrink as you begin to get larger, until you pop outside the crystal and you and the crystal both return to your normal respective sizes.

Our work with crystals is, in the end, another dimension of the search for truth that is our real life's work: to find the jewel within ourselves, symbolized in some belief systems as the jewel in the centre of the lotus flower – the Jewel of Truth. At one level a jewel is a thing which is hard, fixed and immutable. It is an appropriate symbol. A jewel is composed of many facets, of many reflections, each one mirroring the constantly changing patterns of light and colour that surround it. So too is our experience of truth. It is constantly changing, as the world around us changes. And yet that which reflects it, the One Truth, the oneness of all things, is always constant, fixed, immutable.

Thus may our inner truth reflect the constantly changing patterns of our own lives. Life is an adventure; it is an exploration of what is, and what may be. What your life will be in the future is only a reflection of what it is now, and the decisions and actions that you take now. Thus, it is constantly changing and shifting – a constant series of new reflections, reverberating from your own personal inner truth, the truth of God within you.

Let the Crystal Mirror reveal that truth to you.

REFERENCES AND
Further
Reading

Ted Andrews, *How to Read the Aura* (St Paul: Llewellen, 1998)

Ronald Bonewitz with Lilian Verner-Bonds, *New Cosmic Crystals* (London: Thorsons, 2000)

Joseph Campbell, *The Power of Myth* (London: Doubleday, 1988)

Edward S. Dana, *Dana's Textbook of Mineralogy*, 4th edn, edited by W.E. Ford (New York: John Wiley, 1982)

John Harrison, M.D., *Love Your Disease* (London: Angus and Robertson, 1984)

Richard Moss, M.D., *The I That is We* (Berkeley: Celestial Arts, 1981)

Lilian Verner-Bonds, *The Complete Book of Color Healing* (London: Godsfield, 2000)

For further reading on colour and colour healing, see also:

Lilian Verner-Bonds, *Colour Healing* (London: Godsfield, 2000)

Lilian Verner-Bonds with Joseph Corvo, *The Healing Power of Colour and Zone Therapy* (London: Piatkus, 1997)

To contact Lilian Verner-Bonds, write to:

The Colour-Bonds Association
137 Hendon Lane
London N3 3PR
United Kingdom

Other Books by Ronald A.L. Bonewitz

Cosmic Crystals (Thorsons, 1983)

The Cosmic Crystal Spiral (Element Books, 1986)

The Pulse of Life (Element Books, 1987)

The Crystal Heart (Thorsons, 1989)

The Timeless Wisdom of the Egyptians (Hodder & Stoughton Educational, 1998)

The Maya Prophecies (Piatkus, 1999)

A Beginners Guide to Pyramids (Hodder & Stoughton Educational, 1999)

The Wisdom of the Maya, a Maya Oracle (Eddison-Sadd, 2000)

New Cosmic Crystals (Thorsons, 2000)

The Timeless Wisdom of the Maya (Hodder & Stoughton Educational, 2000)

Teach Yourself Egyptian and Mayan Hieroglyphics (Hodder & Stoughton Educational, 2000)